# *The* Gold Mine
## *To Consciousness*

### The missing secrets to self-love and empowered relationships

### Rosemary Bennett

Published by The Psychonomist

Copyright © 2022. All rights reserved. No portion of this publication may be used, reproduced or transmitted by any means, digital, electronic, mechanical, photocopy or recording without written permission of the publisher, except in the case of brief quotations within critical articles or reviews.

ISBN: 978-0-6453598-0-0 (paperback)
ISBN: 978-0-6453598-1-7 (e-book)

First edition, 2022

For book orders and enquiries or to book a personal online appointment, contact: rosemary@thepsychonomist.com.au

 A catalogue record for this book is available from the National Library of Australia

# DEDICATION

This book is dedicated to the Infinite Love within each of us that is ours to find, nurture and give out to all those that we encounter along our life journey.

# ACKNOWLEDGEMENTS

I am so grateful to all the formal teachers that have imparted their incredible knowledge to me through the courses they have so skilfully crafted and taught throughout my life.

I would like to thank all the informal teachers who have crossed my path, friends, relations, class mates, even strangers, literally every person I have encountered in my life has given me the opportunity to look within and develop myself at a soul level.

I would like to thank all the brave souls, who have taken themselves on, in their life and trusted me to assist them with their life journey, by looking within and exploring their inner world, finding the love and light that they are and shining it out into the world. For that I thank you.

# TESTIMONIALS FROM CLIENTS

I have had the pleasure of many interactions with Rosemary over the last decade. These moments have been paramount to my learning and developing choices across my life to date, both professionally and personally. Of late, the awareness that life is the lesson - all aspects of life (I love learning) has meant that I meet each day, the hurdles and accomplishments with curiosity and wonder and am all the better at being human as a result.

I recently read: "It's your identity that shapes your world. The universe reflects back who you are" Vishen Lakiani. Rosemary has been reminding me of this for years.

*Casey Beaumont, Osteopath and business owner at Resilient Health, Adelaide South Australia*

I highly recommend Rosemary and her BodyTalk/Psychonomy sessions. She has been so incredible at helping me to see life in a new perspective. I view my life lessons as a gift that I have asked for and the more that I accept them openly, the more I actualise my human potential. I feel like I have grown in so many ways both mentally and spiritually. She is truly so amazing and I am so grateful that I have someone so knowledgeable, passionate and genuine to help me develop in life. I highly recommend her services to anyone.

*Alana Koufalakis, owner and Beauty Consultant at Diamond Physique, Adelaide South Australia*

Rosemary Bennett is a wonderful practitioner with many remarkable talents and skills on her tool belt.

I have worked in the field of mental health and illness, Psychodynamics and human flourishing, bodywork and the spiritual movement for over 40 years now and over time you garner some very special people that become your own regular practitioners you go to for balance, healing and maintenance. Rosemary is one of these for me and I highly recommend her to anyone who is wanting relief and change in any aspect of their physical, emotional, psychological and spiritual realms which of course are all interwoven anyway.

Her BodyTalk and Psychonomy are fast, effective and life changing. Do yourself a favour your system will love you for it.

*Prue Blackmore, R.N. [psych], Dip Developmental Psych, Dip Shamanic Practice, Dip Transpersonal Counselling, Dip Transpersonal Art Therapy*

As a natural and complimentary medicine practitioner, I found my world becoming complex and intense. I feel the universe has sent Rosemary to help me decipher and unlock my potential. Rosemary's sessions are more than counselling.

Rosemary's counselling ability goes way beyond the emotional but deeper into the experiences we live through and has helped me as part of a deeper and reflective journey into myself. I can't begin to explain how valuable I have found Rosemary's sessions.

I highly recommend this service.

*Michelle Crone, Naturopath*

Rosemary is my 'GO TO' person when I have something going on in my 'self' (body/mind/spirit) that is persistent, or trying to tell me something and I'm not sure exactly what. With Rosemary's 'BodyTalk' modality, I feel like I can keep on top of my own health and healing in a way that is really aligned with me! She works directly with me and my soul energy, and is always completely on point with what is needed.

Through Rosemary's sessions I always gain great healing, understanding and acknowledgement, and I am very grateful for her service, as she is a great ally to my overall health and wellbeing.

Thank you so much Rosemary, you are direct, truthful and hold space with great love and presence, thank you for your ongoing support of me via these sessions.

*Tanya Wilson, Counsellor, Life Coach and Massage Therapist*

Rosemary Bennett is an amazing woman who defies logic with her knowledge and wisdom, anyone who is lucky enough to be blessed with her presence will certainly change your outlook on life to a positive one. Rosemary is my guardian angel helping me through the ups and downs on what life throws at us all, the best way to describe Rosemary is that the beauty is not only her presence but deep down she genuinely cares who sits in front of her. I will never forget how she helped me through the darkest days and held my hand leading the way to a positive light.

Thank you Rosemary for all that you have done and all that you will continue to do.

Rosemary Bennett in one word "AMAZING" enough said.
*Phillip de Pinto, Director and CEO of Universal Motors Auctions, Co-Founder and Chair of Living Without Limits Foundation*

# CONTENTS

Introduction ............................................................. xiii
1. Who and what are we? ........................................... 1
2. The story ............................................................... 7
3. Lessons and the mirror ......................................... 11
4. Relationships, limerence and co-dependence ...... 21
5. How do we know what our lessons are? ............. 25
6. How the way we are born contributes
   to the patterns in our life .................................... 31
7. Drug addiction, drugs and the emotions they suppress ... 63
8. How we learn through opposites ......................... 73
9. The little voice technique and the breath ........... 79
10. We like to be right ................................................ 85
11. How we attach emotions to our mental thoughts
    triggered by our past ........................................... 91
12. Mistakes ................................................................ 97
13. Supply and demand .............................................. 99
14. Depression, anxiety and the moment ................ 103
15. Vehicle versus vehicle ......................................... 113

16. Disease and how we make ourself sick ........................ 117
17. Death, dying and dis-ease ................................................ 123
18. Detachment.......................................................................... 125
19. Can't give from an empty cup......................................... 129
20. The beaker and change..................................................... 133
21. A small internal change can create
    a big external result......................................................... 137
22. Bullies and those that they bully.................................... 141
23. Verbal abuse and bullying................................................ 149
24. The destructiveness of external competition ................ 153
25. What someone else thinks of us is
    none of our business........................................................ 157
26. The circle of influence and the circle of concern .......... 161
27. Communication, the written and spoken word
    and body language........................................................... 165
28. Creating better sleep ......................................................... 169
29. Life is a game...................................................................... 173
30. The block of wood ............................................................. 177
31. How to manifest an amazing future............................... 179
32. How to love ourself ........................................................... 185
33. True service......................................................................... 193
Conclusion.................................................................................. 197
Appendix..................................................................................... 201

# INTRODUCTION

This book has been in development for a very long time, really my whole life. In its pages are learnings and teachings that I have experienced, both personally and professionally, through my own life experiences and through study and education in many different areas, along with each client and the journey they are undertaking. It feels like it has come out of a necessity from working with many clients, who have allowed me the privilege of assisting them to actualise their human potential, which is an ongoing journey. This book has been written for all ages from teenagers all the way through to those of more mature years. Over the last 15 years, the processes I take my clients through have evolved, with the addition of new techniques and information, building a deeper shift in the psyche as the alignment of new information and processes transforms their self-awareness and consciousness to a higher level. I love how each of the techniques I use and the information that each client uncovers align, providing evidence to the client, showing them their patterns and lessons that they are here to let go of. I show people what causes their low energy levels, disease and their negative behaviours and how to raise their energy levels and let go of negativity that doesn't serve them for their highest good. I look at who we are from a scientific view point, as well as, through the human experience. Nothing is an accident or coincident!

Within the pages are learnings from those that I have guided to shift their consciousness from outside of themselves to an internal view, so they see life from a new perspective, giving them the knowledge and confidence to make empowering choices in their life. When we have the tools and the knowledge of how to let go of negative thoughts and emotions and the patterns that created them, it is amazing what life and the relationships we have can look like when we have a new way of seeing ourself in the world.

## How to use this book

I have taken the processes that I guide my client's through in the first session and subsequent sessions and transformed it into the written word. In parts it is asking the reader to look at their life and write what they find, so they can see patterns and lessons and where they come from. They may need to gather some information from others, so they can look more deeply at how and what they need to work on within themselves. Some of the parts of the process that are more individual, such as someone's numerological and North Node information that I use are unable to be shared in this format and can be delved into more deeply in an individual personal session with me.

I have written the book from an inclusive perspective, using the words ourself, ourselves, we and our, rather than you, your and yourself. I only use 'you' or 'your' when asking a question. Many people when talking about themselves say "you" rather than "I", "we" or "our". To own our words and be empowered, rather than being a victim of our life, expressing "I" when we mean ourself, creates more power in what we say, we are owning what we say and what we are communicating. I am inviting the reader to look within themselves, delve deeply and come out the other side with a new perspective of who and what they are. As the book is read take what works and leave what doesn't, we all have choice and free will.

This book can also be used on a daily basis, by opening to a chapter and reading it, using it as reminder to continue to love ourselves in each moment.

We are all part of humanity and our consciousness is a part of the collective unconscious of all, which means as we shift our own consciousness, we are shifting humanity as a collective.

Chapter 1

# WHO AND WHAT ARE WE?

Who are you really? What do you think of yourself and how much do you contemplate the deeper parts of yourself? How unconscious are you in your own life, your inner life? I see many people spending most of their time thinking about how their external environment and their relationships effect how they are seen in the world and how they feel about themselves and how others treat them. This can create feelings of fear, anxiety, depression, anger, resentment, guilt, sadness and many other negative emotions. We can become powerless when our external world and the relationships we have, have more to say about who we are, than how we think, feel and see ourself.

My endeavour is to give a new way to look at ourselves, in our life, so we operate from a different paradigm, enabling us to be the conductor of our own life.

What if I said we have a physical body, but we are much more than our physical body because we have awareness that we have a body. Our awareness of our physical body tells us that we cannot be just a physical body. If we were only a body, we would not be aware of it, we would be it and have no awareness of anything else. We are aware when our body has been hurt or has a disease and we feel pain. We are aware when our body does not work properly. We know how to make our body move, we control where we take it, how we move it and what we put in it. We have awareness when our body is sick (most of the time) and recognise symptoms. So how can we only be our body? It is our consciousness, our awareness of our body that tells us we are more than our physical body.

Let's look further. We all have emotions, both positive and negative, emotions we like to feel and emotions we would rather not. We often get caught up in the negative emotions we feel and think we are the emotions, that the emotions are us and see no way of getting rid of the unwanted emotions. It feels like we are the emotions.

Because we know what we are feeling we can't be the emotion. We are more than the emotion because we know what emotions we are feeling (most of the time), we know when we are feeling sad, we know when we are feeling anxious, we know when we are feeling guilty, we know what we are feeling in every moment. We can name it, sadness, anxiety, anger, jealousy etc. If we realise that we are not the emotion and move our awareness away from the emotion and become the observer of the emotion, the emotion usually lessons and sometimes disappears. If we know what we are feeling how can we be the emotion? We have emotions but we are not our emotions because we can, when conscious and self-aware, separate ourself from the emotions. We have an emotional body, a body of emotions. Our awareness of our emotions means we must be more than our emotions. We have consciousness that allows us to step away from the emotion when we realise, we are not the emotion.

Let's say our name without speaking, say it in our head, think our name. Did you hear yourself say your name? If you didn't try again. Did you hear it this time? We are hearing ourself think our name. Who was listening, our ears did not hear anything because we did not say our name out loud? Someone heard us say our name. We have mental thoughts but we are not our mental thoughts because we can have self-awareness of the thoughts we are thinking. We know what we are thinking so how can we be the thought? How often does the same mental thought repeat over and over again? We have a body of mental thoughts, a mental body. We often are not conscious about what we are thinking, we think we are the thoughts. It is our thoughts that determine what we think about and often they seem to take over our life. We then attach emotions, both positive and negative to those thoughts. When the thoughts and emotions are negative, we start a chain of events that are unhealthy and detrimental to our life. We can't have a thought without an emotion or an emotion without a thought. We usually use our mental and emotional bodies together, especially when we do not have self-awareness and consciousness of who and what we really are. Over time the process of negative thoughts and emotions can impact the physical body making it tired and exhausted and eventually creating disease. It takes a lot more energy to hold on to a negative thought than a positive one. Think of friends or family members that are very negative, they are often unwell and low in energy. How healthy are you, in your physical, emotional and mental bodies? How much energy do you have?

If we are not our physical body, our emotions or our mental thoughts, who are we? Who was listening to us think our name?

We are more than who we think we are. We have consciousness. We can be conscious of ourself, our thoughts, our emotions and our physical bodies. With self-awareness we can use our consciousness to watch ourself, in our life, like we are behind the camera watching the making of a movie, the movie of our life. We are the director of our own life. We are often unaware of the true role we play in our own life. We can separate ourself from the thoughts that are negative and make better choices about what we want to think. We can choose not to attach negative emotions to those thoughts, we do have choice. When self-aware and conscious, we can become the observer of our thoughts and emotions, we can observe ourself in our life. We, as the observer, through conscious awareness, become the creator of our reality. We are, and have a consciousness, (a soul some may call it).

The Science of Quantum Mechanics tells us we are energy that appears to have a physical body because it is observed. We are made up of atoms and our atoms are made up of vortices of energy that are constantly spinning and vibrating. We are really beings of energy and vibration which creates a frequency. As we focus closer and closer on the structure of the atom, we would see nothing, we would observe a physical void. We are made up of invisible energy, not tangible matter. Energy can't be destroyed, so if we are energy, we continue to exist in an energetic form after we leave our physical body at our death. Our consciousness goes on forever.

Nikola Tesla states "If you want to know the secrets of the universe, think in terms of energy, frequency and vibration". A fundamental conclusion of the new physics acknowledges that the observer creates their reality. As observers we are personally involved with the creation of our own reality. Physicists are being forced to admit that the universe is "mental construction". When an atom changes its state, it absorbs or emits electromagnetic frequencies, this is what changes it's state. We now know that different states of emotion, perception and feeling, result in different electromagnetic frequencies. What we think and feel and how we perceive our experiences not only effects ourself but it also creates an impact in our external environment and the relationships we have in it.

Our thoughts, feelings and emotions create our own unique energy signature, positive thoughts create a higher level of energy, and a higher vibration, resulting in a higher frequency. Our thoughts affect much more than most people realise including what diseases we experience.

# THE GOLD MINE TO CONSCIOUSNESS

For what reason would we choose to come into a physical body and have a human life experience? Why are we here on the planet in a body? Let's look a little deeper.

Nothing is conscious everything is energy – Scientists explain the world of Quantum Physics by consciousreminder found on the net.

Chapter 2

# THE STORY

I am going to tell a story, a story that may seem a little strange to some and quite acceptable and normal to others. While reading this story think about our own life story.

Before I came on the planet, into a body, I was a very eager soul (consciousness). I was ready to take on a human body, again, for furthering my soul's evolution. I knew (at a soul level) that taking on a body was the process for me to learn and evolve.

There was a big board with lots of lessons on it, I chose plenty and lots of hard ones. I chose those that were to assist me in my next level of soul growth. I wrote out a contract with myself, agreeing to learn the chosen lessons to the best of my ability as a human being. I didn't choose anything I was incapable of doing.

To learn we need experiences and to have experiences we need an environment to have them in. We also need to experience relationships with others in that environment to learn and develop ourself. I looked down on the planet and asked myself where do I need to live to give me the best opportunities to learn the lessons I chose and what kind of people do I need in that environment?

I chose an environment that was a little isolated on a farm, that is where I was going to start my life. I chose a father and a mother who had behaviours and ways of being both positive and negative that would be perfect for me to learn my lessons. I also chose an older brother and to be the baby of the family. Once the choice was made it was time for me to come into the body I had chosen, knowing that it too would be the perfect body for me to learn my chosen lessons in, and so I was born and had the perfect birth to assist in the setting up of my behaviours and patterns that would serve me for my lessons. I remembered nothing of my choices as I came into the world.

As I grew up, I started to notice what I didn't like about my environment and those that were in it. Why did my father and mother hit me, people who loved me shouldn't hit me? Why did my mother do lots of things for me, cooked, sewed my clothes, took me to all my sports games but seemed to be lacking warmth, instead having a coldness about her sometimes, where was the gentleness and kindness, everything was so serious? Why was I not allowed to express myself when I was angry, instead told off and sent to my room? Why was my brother so different to me, why did we fight most of the time? How could we be born to the same parents yet be so different? Why did I have two great friends throughout my school years and everybody else seemed to like me one day and dislike me the next, poking me, pushing me around, calling me names, I felt so ostracised? Why did my grade five teacher call me 'busybody Bennett' in front of the whole class all year? I just wanted to help people. Why don't my relationships with men work, why are they so hard to have? The questions went on and on and as I got older with no understanding of the reasons behind the experiences, I felt like, life itself, was beating me up.

How many of you can relate to or add your own harsh realities of life as you were growing up? How many of you are still having a life that feels like it is beating you up?

I always had an enquiring mind and wanted answers so as I got older, I started to look at my life and the relationships I had and after some intense inward journeying and a lot of formal study, I found a new way to look at my life that was much more empowering and made a lot more sense to me.

Now if my story was true, that we set up, before we come into a body, negative unconscious patterns of behaviour that create our beliefs and our environment and the people in it, to assist us to learn the lessons we choose, who would be responsible for our life? **We** would be responsible because it was **our** choice. It is how we give ourself the opportunity to become conscious and self-aware.

As we move through life, no one forces us to stay in a relationship, no one forces us take that drink or drug, no one forces us to take that job, we choose, often through beliefs and filters we are unaware of and reasons we can't explain. It is the lessons we choose before we are born, that set up the experiences and relationships we encounter in our life, to give us the opportunity to evolve. Much of what we experience in our life, I believe, is pre-ordained because of the lessons we have chosen, which means that we would always be in the right place, at the right time, doing the right thing, placing ourselves in experiences which create opportunities to learn the lessons we chose to learn, in a body, as a human being. Which means whether our life feels great or not so great, it is perfect in that moment. Our lessons don't come in pretty pink boxes with a pretty pink bow, their intensity grows and grows if we ignore them, until we become conscious and learn them.

When life is going well, do we ever step outside our comfort zone, push ourself to grow or change? Usually not. I find when life is going well most people resist change because they want everything to stay just as it is. It is the turbulence, the disruptions, the dramas and the challenging times in our life, where we are given the opportunities to learn and complete a lesson. The timing of events and experiences are perfect because we are all connected and we assist each other, with the lessons that we chose, until we learn them.

Which way of looking at our life has the most power, the victim, blaming others for our circumstances or taking responsibility and owning our journey and the experiences we choose to have in it, even though many of our choices appear unconscious.

Let's look at how we give our self the opportunity to change, adapt and grow.

# Chapter 3

# LESSONS AND THE MIRROR

If life is about learning let's look at how the lessons that we chose are going to show up in our lives.

Write down what the relationship was like with our mother when we were under ten and then in our teenage years. The relationship is with the person that represented the mother figure in our life. It may have been a stepmother or grandmother if our mother passed over or was not in our life. It may be both the biological mother and a step mother or a mother through adoption, in this case write down each relationship separately.

What kind of mother was she? Did she work or was she a 'stay at home' mother? Was she caring and nurturing, was she strict or moody? Was she available or unavailable emotionally? Would she listen to what the problem was and show understanding and gently give advice or did she say 'you will be ok' or not want to listen and push aside the issue? Did she do everything for everyone else and put herself last? Did she suffer from depression or anxiety? Was she the boss in the house or more subservient? Could you talk to her would she listen or just tell you what to do? Was she a drug taker, including alcohol and cigarettes? Was there a separation of parents in the home and did that change the behaviour or mood of your mother? What, if any, are the behaviours that irritated you about your mother and possibly still do? Don't be limited by the questions, think outside the box and write what it felt like to be a child around the mother figure. This is not to be nasty, especially if our mother has passed on, there is a reason that I am asking these questions that will be explained. Complete this part by writing down all the answers before reading further to fully benefit from this process.

Now do the same with our father or father figure that was present when we were under ten then in our teenage years. What kind of father did you have, kind or strict? Was he absent a lot of the time, working? Did he play with you and share with you and teach you when you were young? Was he more serious or moody? Could you talk to your father was he emotionally available if you had a problem? Did he listen to you or was he authoritarian and bossy? Was he a drug taker, including alcohol and cigarettes? Was he absent through separation or divorce, was he a part time father? What things irritated you about your father, his negative behaviour and may possibly still irritate you? Remember don't be limited by the questions whatever is written down is very important. If the father or father figure has passed over, remember these questions are being asked for a very good reason which we will come to shortly. Complete this section before reading on.

Next, do you have a partner, do the same, write about the partner? This can be a husband or wife, same sex partner, boyfriend or girlfriend (if the relationship is new the negative behaviours can be harder to see sometimes, this will be explained in more detail in another chapter). If there isn't a present partner, pick the longest relationship that has been had in the past. Ask the same questions, including what is irritating and annoying about them and don't be limited by the questions. Please complete this part before reading on.

Now there will be three sections, mother, father and partner as a minimum (more if there are step parents etc). More than one partner can be used in this activity.

Once completed **NOW** turn the page.......

Now have a look at what has been written about each person and ask yourself, **who did I marry** (or date) **my mother or father**? Who is my partner most like or are they a bit of both? Look first at the behaviours we do not like in the parent or parents and see if they show up in our partner (particularly if we are struggling with our relationship with our partner). For many it is very clear who they have married and the traits and behaviours are very obvious, for others they need to look harder. We often have to look from an objective place to see this. This may be a new realisation or one that was already realised. It may be a realisation that feels uncomfortable and strange.

Now have a look at previous partners, old boyfriends and girlfriends including previous ex wives and husbands. Previous partners may follow a pattern and be like the same parent as our present partner or we may swap from parent to parent. Let's see the reason that this happens.

Our parents (and our grandparents, our siblings or step brothers and sisters if we have them) are our spiritual family, we chose them as our teachers, our lesson givers. They are the greatest gift we have, although we may not feel that at this point in our investigation. If we are not very conscious of the bigger picture of our life it may be very challenging to see the gift that our spiritual family is offering us. We choose our parents (and siblings) because they become our perfect mirror as they unconsciously project back at us what we usually need to learn and change about ourself. The projection (or mirror) can be a negative or positive trait or behaviour, it can even appear positive but when we look deeper it is a negative behaviour when it comes to loving ourselves, such as a parent who does everything for everybody else and puts themselves last. This can create a lot of resentment in the person, or they may see themselves as a victim because no one does anything for them, which is very unhealthy. Our parents are not doing this consciously, it is because of their ability to mirror our lessons, via their behaviours, that we chose them to be our parents, so they can teach us about ourself and what we have chosen to learn in a physical body, as a human being. This is why they are our greatest gift, as our teachers, to assist us to look inward and discover who and what we really are. Let's look at how this can show up.

If we need to learn to be patient, do we get someone who is patient or impatient to show us how to be patient? Usually, it will be someone who is impatient that shows up, to show us, how to be patient if we are open to learning the lesson. The lesson, via the behaviour we see reflected at us by another, is not usually what we do to others, it is usually what we are unconsciously doing to ourself. In this example of experiencing someone, such as a parent, being impatient, we would look within and ask ourself, 'how patient and kind am I towards myself?' 'Do I expect to get everything right the first time I do it?' Am I impatient with myself as I move through my life wanting to be something or somewhere immediately?'

Another example, if a parent or partner were/are emotionally unavailable, what is the lesson we are needing to learn? We need to ask ourself how emotionally available are we to ourself? If we are not able to get in touch with our own emotions by being open to understanding our feelings and trust what we are feeling and be able to express them out to others, then we will get the reflection back at us from others of emotional unavailability. Many people suppress their emotions with drugs, (including alcohol and cigarettes) which means they do not want to feel their negative emotions (this will be covered in another chapter). The suppression of our emotions makes us emotionally unavailable to ourself.

Our lessons come in many different ways. We either repeat the pattern of a parent or we do the opposite. Both can hold a lesson for us. If we don't learn the lesson our parents (and siblings) are projecting at us then the lesson will continue and show up usually with our partners. This is why, our partners, can start behaving like one (or both) of our parents because we have not learnt the lessons, that originally our parents were unconsciously mirroring at us. In life, anyone can start to reflect back at us an unlearnt lesson, siblings, relations, friends, colleagues and work mates, even those in our community, but I find the strongest and most relevant lessons are from those closest to us being our parents, siblings and partners.

Most lessons being projected at us from our external environment are showing us the destructive way we treat ourself, our inner critic can be really savage and starts when we are very young and never gives up unless we become conscious of the little voice in our head, the one we heard when we thought our name, that little voice, our mental body. We need to be conscious of what our inner voice is telling us about ourselves.

Unless we are conscious of our lessons and how we are behaving in life, the mirroring of the lesson usually gets stronger and stronger. How many times in a family does something that was a small disagreement or a little annoyance grow and become a much bigger issue, sometimes to the point of not speaking at all for years and years, especially between parents and children. Remember we as souls choose the perfect parents and siblings for our lessons, for our growth and development, yet often we blame them for not being what we want them to be. We want them to change. When we spend time looking at what we don't like in a parent, (or a way of being that is not serving the parents to have love for themselves) we get to see what is being reflected at us, so we can change who we are being, our behaviours and see ourself through a more conscious reality. It gives us the opportunity to get what our lesson is from the relationship with our parents and spiritual family. The mirroring of the lesson stops when we learn it and we do not have to have it continue to show up with our parents, partners and other relationships. It is our job to notice, to be aware of ourself in each relationship we have.

When we see a behaviour or way of being in another person being reflected back at us that we do not like, how do we know what the lesson is for ourselves?

Think about the behaviour we do not like in a parent or partner and now look inward at how we treat ourself. Do you treat yourself the same way? For example, we may have a father (or partner) who is very critical of what we are doing or not doing in our life, notice, how do you talk to yourself? Do you criticise yourself about how you look or what you do or don't do in your life, perhaps what you don't have or don't think you deserve? Do you beat yourself up if you fail or can't complete something, or don't think you are as good as others, the list goes on? What does your little voice (your mental body) say to you over and over again? How many times a day does a negative, critical mental thought come in to your mind? Quite often we are unaware that we criticise ourself because we are unconscious of our thoughts and emotions, taking no notice of them, or we blame others not even recognising our own state of mind. Making them conscious gives us the opportunity to work with them and let them go.

The negativity that we hold inwardly about ourself becomes the reflection. If there is criticism coming at us from others it is usually because we are inwardly criticising ourself first. Our parents (and our siblings and partners) are unconsciously doing what we need them to do so we can evolve through learning, growing and developing ourselves from the mirrored lessons. We often incarnate into the same spiritual family over and over again, (we can be very slow at learning).

Many, many times my clients leave, often after only one session and create a whole new relationship with their parents, siblings and partners because they have become conscious of some of the major lessons they are here to learn. They see themselves differently, are kinder and gentler to themselves so those in their environment do not have to reflect some major lessons back at them anymore. It is interesting how the dynamic changes in the relationship as the other person has not become conscious, they did not go and see anybody, the reflection and mirroring just stops or at the very least reduces significantly, much to the amazement of my clients.

When we play the blame game, thinking the issue is outside of ourself and has nothing to do with us, everyone loses, especially ourself. Remember we made the choice to be here, we chose those that would be perfect to be the teachers of our life lessons, we are responsible for our life, we create it with every choice we make and continue to make.

When we take responsibility for our life and the experiences we have in our life, we are empowering ourselves and generally have much better outcomes to situations that we have attracted to ourselves, for our self-development and learning. Our new awareness and consciousness of who we are being, in any situation, gives us a better outcome.

If a lot of our learning come via our relationships let's look at them more closely.

Chapter 4

# RELATIONSHIPS, LIMERENCE AND CO-DEPENDENCE

Most relationships are co-dependent. When we first meet someone, particularly intimate partners, they seem so lovely, caring, kind, thoughtful, they will go above and beyond to make us happy, as we will do for them. This is called Limerence. Limerence can last for only a few months or for a number of years. During the limerence phase there are no lessons being projected back at us, the relationship works well. The other person can do no wrong they appear to be perfect, (well almost perfect). We sometimes are aware of little signs, that are just under the surface, that feel uncomfortable but we ignore them because most of the relationship is working. Sometimes we don't see anything negative. This feels like love and we move the relationship forward to the next stage.

Over time relationships develop and become deeper often eventually leading to marriage or living together.

At some point in the relationship and it is different for everybody, the limerence stops and the projections of our unlearnt lessons start. Most relationships become co-dependent because of the mirroring and projections of lessons that we are still to learn, that we did not learn with our primary lesson givers, our parents and siblings.

We start to see traits and behaviours we don't like or that trigger us and we react, usually over react, rather than respond to the experiences we are having with our partner. The mirroring of the unlearnt lessons has started. Unless we are conscious that this is what is happening, life can become very unpleasant. The longer it takes each person, in the relationship, to see the reflected lessons that are being reflected unconsciously by the other person, the more the relationship deteriorates.

When we first met our partner, if they had shown up with all the traits and behaviours that we now don't like would we have ever dated them? The answer is usually no, we wouldn't have had anything to do with them. Without limerence we would possibly not date anyone. Limerence allows us to form the relationships we need to have in our life, to give ourselves the opportunity to learn the lessons we have chosen. We attract (unconsciously choose) the perfect relationships we need for our lessons. The relationships we have, I feel, are pre-ordained they are not accidental or a coincidence, they are perfectly timed throughout our life for our growth and development. We create them unconsciously.

It is interesting to look at marriage, the signing of the marriage certificate. When we sign a marriage certificate, we become family, we usually take the others name and we are now a part of each other's family. I often find that the mirroring magnifies when the relationship is formalised by marriage. Who has heard of the couples that have been living happily together for sometimes up to 20 years and then they choose to marry and don't last a year? This is an extreme example of what happens when we become family, the projections and mirroring can appear, or become stronger, and creates the opportunity to learn our lessons. The mirroring and projections are a consequence of the lessons we chose to learn in a human life.

Projections are not done consciously by a person, it is unconscious. We have asked them to assist us with the lessons we chose before we took on a body, they are doing what we asked them to do for our growth and soul development, as we are doing for them. Once we learn what we need to change about ourself inwardly, the external projections stop. I have witnessed this many, many times with my clients. After they shift their consciousness and awareness from outside themselves to a more internal perspective at the first appointment, (for some it takes longer) they start coming to future appointments saying that their father, mother, siblings or partner have stopped doing behaviours that they disliked. They have shifted their consciousness, letting go of negative ways of behaviour towards themselves and tell me they now have the best relationship they have ever had with those they love. A big part of this is because they have acquired a higher level of self love and self-awareness and that is now being reflected back at them.

Being conscious and aware of ourselves, our inner feelings and thoughts about ourself, including our beliefs, assists us to see the lessons easier and often quicker before they take over our life. I love working with young people because they don't have years of beliefs and behaviours, so they shift really quickly, giving them a totally new direction in their life.

How do we know what lessons we have chosen to learn? When working with a client I use several ways to show them what their lessons could be. Let's look at what they are.

Chapter 5

# HOW DO WE KNOW WHAT OUR LESSONS ARE?

The lessons we choose to learn can be challenging to find unless we are conscious. By becoming conscious we are generally more open to seeing ourself in our life and what our lessons are. I view my clients from an esoteric (unseen) aspect. I look at the unseen, what is hidden at a deep level and bring it to the surface and work with it. What I have found is the tools and modalities I use uncover and show what is already there, giving evidence of the patterns and behaviours, negative mental thoughts and emotions that cause our own downfall and make our life difficult. With an understanding of the causes, we can let go of them and create a different reality.

Using the reflected lessons from parents, siblings and partners, I show how they align with the behaviours and patterns formed by where the North and South Nodes are in a client's astrological chart. I work with Numerology, related to a client's name and birth date, along with the patterns formed from the in utero and physical birth experience and where they are placed by their birth amongst their siblings, plus any diseases and drug they use. By bringing many different aspects of a person's life together, I find evidence of underlying negative patterns and behaviours that prevent a person from reaching their human potential. By creating a new perspective of themselves in their life they have the potential to manifest an amazing life.

I am not an astrologer but when working with a client I use a fabulous book by Jan Spiller, Astrology for the Soul. This book focusses on the North and South Nodes of the moon called the Nodal axis of the chart. It is calculated from our birthdate which tells us which astrological sign our Nodes are in when we were born.

Our South Node and what Zodiac sign it is in when we were born can show us what ways of being don't work for us. The North node gives us ways of being that assist us to excel and create balance in our life. It is interesting how accurate the tendencies to leave behind are for my clients. Many a time, as I read the list to them, they agree with me that this is how they are in life. I see many of the lessons my clients have in their life are expressed in their South Node. With new awareness it is easier to see ourselves in our life, as the observer, rather than being so 'in it', where we don't see what negative behaviours and habits we are exhibiting.

Our North node is one way that shows us what we have come here to learn and what to work towards to improve our life.

The attributes to develop are often the opposite to what is not working for us. There is much to discover about ourself through our North and South nodes and also our family members, partners and children. Remember we are all here learning and mirroring each other's lessons. Having knowledge on what others are learning can assist us to understand and create better relationships for everyone, especially parents and children.

Astrology for the Soul: Jan Spiller

Another tool I use is Numerology. Numerology is the science of numbers and their vibrational qualities. Each letter of the alphabet has a numerological number that is associated with it and each of the numbers have qualities both positive and negative that show us the blue print of our life. Our date of birth when combined with our name gives us a map of our soul's journey to evolution. Each person's Numerology is unique to them. We are all unique and individual with our personal blueprint that is established before we are born and confirmed at our birth.

Adding to the techniques and tools I look at the way we were born. As a trained rebirther and breath worker I have also seen the patterns of behaviour that are created by the experience we undertake at our birth. How we are physically born is perfect, it aligns with our lessons. Our birth experience, sets up patterns in our life which relate to the lessons we have chosen, nothing is left out, it all aligns. We seem to be exceptional at creating experiences in our life for the growth and evolution of our soul and the human race.

I look at a client's medical history, the diseases they have had and those they are dealing with when they come to see me, plus what drugs they have used and are still using.

It is interesting, how each of the different modalities I use to view a client's life, tells a very similar story of what they are struggling with and the changes that would assist them to create a better life. A picture starts to form and as soon as the client shifts their awareness and consciousness to look within, the faster they let go of old patterns and create a more balanced enjoyable life.

At this point, I incorporate The BodyTalk System which is a form of energy work that allows the body's energy systems to be resynchronised so they can operate as nature intended. The body is a dynamic, interactive, interdependent network of energy matrixes, consciousness and physical function. The BodyTalk system is designed to harmonise the different forms of energy frequencies to optimise the overall balance in the body at all levels, physical, emotional, mental and spiritual.

Something new to my tool kit is Nutripuncture which works at a cellular level, assisting the body to self-regulate. It uses electromagnetic pathways, via trace minerals to convey information to specific areas of the body, including our internal organs. It creates, maintains, regulates and optimises the balance of the vital currents in relation to the body's five senses, which is how we see, hear, touch, taste and smell. The five senses are our reality of how life is. Our five senses are how we look at ourself in the world, our environment and those in it.

Health and wellness with Nutripuncture<br>BodyTalk Fundamentals: Dr. John Veltheim and Sylvia Muizniels.<br>IBA Global Healing. International BodyTalk Association Florida USA

I am always looking for new techniques and therapies to enhance a person's ability to actualise their human potential. I continue to add new information as we are forever evolving.

I combine as many different skills, techniques and tools as possible to show a client their patterns so they can make them conscious and let them go. Let's look at how our birth process creates patterns of behaviour in our life that don't serve us in a positive way and how they can connect into the negative behaviours.

Chapter 6

# HOW THE WAY WE ARE BORN CONTRIBUTES TO THE PATTERNS IN OUR LIFE

If all experiences are an opportunity for us to learn about ourself and let go of what does not serve us for our highest potential as a human being, where do many of our patterns of negative behaviour start?

Through spending years as a Rebirther and Breath Worker and a BodyTalk therapist, I have witnessed the influences that the womb experience, the way we are physically born and the first minutes after our birth, have on how we move through life and the negative patterns of behaviours we have.

Each of our cells has a memory of all of its experiences and as a cell multiplies the cellular memory, continues into the new cells, which means we can carry all of our experiences positive and negative, consciously or unconsciously, with us forever, unless those memories are released out of the cells. What we think (our beliefs) and the emotions we attach to those thoughts, when negative, will eventually manifest in the body as disease. Some of our thoughts and beliefs come from the in-utero, birthing and newborn experience.

The birthing process can be very traumatic for the baby (even if considered normal) as it moves from the womb, through the birth canal and out into the harsh world. The baby may not even get to enter the birth canal it may be taken out via a planned or emergency caesarean. We make unconscious decisions related to what survival means to us and those decisions become our "personal lies or personal laws" (our patterns of behaviour) and continue to affect our relationship with ourself and with others until we clear them.

Birth is life, much of our ability to change (or let go of old patterns and behaviours) comes from understanding the relationship between our birth and the patterns it created and release the cellular memory from the in utero and birth experience. By learning about our birth process, and the patterns that are formed by the type of birth we had, we can gain insight into how our birth has been influential in forming the very patterns that align with our negative behaviours. These are often the same negative behaviours that show up in our astrological North and South Nodes and our Numerological influences. Once patterns are made conscious, we can create positive changes in our behaviour to enhance our life.

The position we are born in our family, whether it is first born child, second born, third born (it then cycles again, fourth born has first born patterns, fifth born has second born patterns and so on) and only child etc, also determines our social habits and the tasks we are here to undertake, according to the position we chose that is assigned to our destiny. Our family constellation contributes to the structure of our emotions and how we react to life situations. When we let go of (or have them removed through BodyTalk or rebirthing) the patterns and beliefs, conscious or unconscious, that create difficulties in our relationships, especially the relationship we have with ourself, we have the opportunity to learn new empowering ways of behaving that create better health and strengthen our love for ourself and others. This in turn creates stronger more empowering and loving relationships.

We choose the perfect birth for ourself. It is so interesting how many parents plan what they want for the birth of their baby and when the time comes for the birth, the plans go out the window and the baby is born exactly how the baby chooses to be born, creating the perfect patterning, to be made conscious, so it can be released as part of our life experiences.

The following types of births are taken directly from Robyn Fernance's book, Being Born (How your birth affects your learning performance, lifestyle and relationships). Robyn's book goes into details about each type of birth, I have included only a part of the summery of each birth type. For those looking to delve more deeply into the birth patterns I have included in the Appendix where the book can be purchased.

When reading the different types of births, take into consideration, that the birth process would most likely include more than one of the below scripts, meaning that they may overlap. This means that some of the patterns of behaviour in one birth script may be stronger than in another or may not resonate at all.

There are more unconscious patterns and conditions from ones in utero, birth and newborn experience that are not covered here, it is a big subject full of many possibilities. I hope that this information assists in furthering the depth to which each reader looks within themselves to discover and let go of old limiting beliefs and behaviours.

Take the list and ask both parents, if you are able to, what type of birth you had. The list can be read out to them and they will respond to which types were relevant at your birth. Questions like 'was I wanted?' can be challenging sometimes for a parent to answer. Explain to them that being honest is more helpful than evading or lying about how they felt when they found out they were expecting a baby. Letting our parents know we choose how we are born and we chose them to be our parents can ease their concerns of upsetting us. If a history of our birth can not be established read through the chapter and as it is being read if a way of being born resonates with the challenges and behaviours faced by the reader it most likely means that birth type is how the birth was.

# Types of Birth Scripts

1. Big Baby Births
2. Born in the Sac Births
3. Breech Births
4. Caesarean - Emergency Births
5. Caesarean – Planned Births
6. 'Conditions of the Mother' Births
7. Cord around the Neck Births
8. Drugged Births
9. Easy Births
10. Fast Births
11. Forceps Delivered Births
12. Held Back Births
13. Induced Births
14. Late Births
15. Near to Death Births
16. Normal Births
17. Premature Births
18. Turned at Birth
19. Twins (Multiple Births)
20. Unwanted Births
21. Wrong Sex Births

## 1. Big Baby Births

- They will tend to have big ideas, yet they seem not to be able to fulfill them.
- They can outgrow the space/relationship they are in.
- They may find themselves disappointed with the 'littleness' and limitations of others.
- They love developing ideas, yet may not always be happy with the outcome.
- They have a tendency to hold back for fear of hurting others.
- They may experience inner conflict when thinking small to please others.

### Why choose to be a big baby

- To be well nourished by what is available.
- To learn patience and tolerance when others and circumstances do not fit into life easily.
- To allow others to experience their pain, you are innocent.
- To be pleased with your development and see positive rewards resulting from it.
- To concentrate on moving forward regardless of any obstacles and delays, even if it is your negative thinking. Move beyond it and find ways the environment can work with you rather that against you.

## 2. Born in the sack births

- It may take considerable effort to trust others to take care of themselves.
- Being vulnerable to psychic attack, they could feel they need protection to feel safe.
- Separation as a means for safety from others and from what is 'out there' could be used.
- They could go into 'psychic shock' when something unforeseen happens.
- They may feel betrayed by others when going through change.
- They could be 'on guard' and in control of what needs to happen for them rather than surrender to the higher plan of things.

### Why choose to be a born in the sac birth

- To remember how easy it is to be here.
- To psychically stay intact no matter what happens around you.
- To know how to carry your safety with you when change is taking place.
- To remember how well you keep a connection between worlds.
- To release the fear of your greatness by acting out your gift.

- To trust yourself to 'tune-in' to what is good for you and others.
- To know that you are psychically safe.
- To reinforce your ability to be here whole and complete in all bodies, physically, mentally, emotionally, spiritually and psychically.

## 3. Breach births

- They could feel they are always doing it differently to others.
- They may feel stuck in going the way they want to go.
- They frequently find their viewpoint is opposite to others.
- What is right for others does not seem right for them.
- To be stubbornly wanting their own way even if it is harder and hurts more.
- Tend to set up many options for themselves, not really knowing the best one to choose.
- They could find themselves with family/friends who want to do the choosing for them.
- May make life hard for themselves by getting 'stuck' in situations they do not seem to be able to find their way out of easily.

### Why choose to be a breach birth

- To be different and know that you have your own unique way.
- To feel past fear when you head towards unknown areas.

- To be loved and accepted regardless of your choices.
- To know there could be peaceful, easy options in achieving what you want.
- To learn to seek help if you are feeling you are losing your way.
- To demonstrate alternative ways of doing things that others may perceive to be hard or long.
- To think on your feet, walk your talk and let the rest of yourself follow.

## 4. Caesarean – emergency births

- Could be strong minded about their way being the right way.
- May be fearful that their rite of passage is unrecognised.
- Could be often distracted or side-tracked from set tasks and leave work unfinished.
- Their great desire usually is to find that <u>one</u> task that completes them.
- They could tend to have a sense of failure compared to others, yet may excel at tasks not coped with by others.
- Could have an extra sense about things happening to them that is not 'normal'.
- They have a tendency to panic over small disturbances as well as become frantic when things seem to be getting more complicated.
- Tendency to crave affection and need lots of loving and cuddles.

- Could appear over dependent and needy, never really knowing how to say good-bye and be unattached and usually do it by causing something 'big' to disconnect them and then refuse any nurturing or physical contact at all.

**Why choose to be a caesarean emergency birth**

- To know there is a creative way to short cut procedures.
- To love being different from others and succeed at it.
- To accept leadership in an easy upright way and receive recognition for it.
- To demonstrate uniqueness in a compassionate caring way.
- To realise people can assist you in making life easy for you.
- To learn how to keep it simple rather than need complication.
- To recognise you are really loved and to unconditionally love the love given.

## 5. Caesarean – planned births

- May feel over-organised by others to ensure a minimum of fuss and disruption to what is already happening.
- Tend to feel they have to make things convenient for others.

- Could find themselves concerned and worried about how other's lives are to work out before they can focus on and work on their own life.
- May feel things are to planned and not happening naturally enough for them.
- May act subservient and see it as a requirement to follow all the rules and what everyone else wants, or so indoctrinated by the control over their life that they come out as controllers and end up the 'boss' of the family.
- Tend to have feelings of not being worth as much as other things are made out to be.

## Why choose to be a caesarean planned birth

- To do what it takes to be here despite a lot going on.
- To have it easy, painless and all prepared for you.
- To expect the best of everything and be compassionate and loving towards others and what they are going through.
- To love deeply despite all invitations to do otherwise.
- To develop a close connection to what is natural rather than be disconnected and drawn to the unnatural.
- To go beyond the fears and limitations of others and have it easy.
- To keep the high standards and lead with compassion and understanding by 'leading from behind' by creating win/win situations by empowering others.

## 6. 'Conditions of the mother' births

- Could be attracted to people who seem to have something wrong with them all the time.
- May be dependent on another's life working before anything is done about their life.
- Tend to fear for their survival and could fear for the survival of the mother/loved one.
- May become anxious if things are not going right.
- Could have a tendency to feel dumped on when things are not working out well.
- An over concentration on what negatively could go wrong rather than the ease and comfort of what could work.

## Why choose to be a conditions of the mother birth

- To stand in the truth that you make a positive difference and people will benefit in a positive way because you are here.
- To transcend negative conditions and not be distracted by what is negatively going on for others.
- To release co-dependency and not 'have to rely on another' for a life.
- To practice loving detachment and do what it takes to be here joyfully loving life.
- To release any guilt and get on with enjoying you full self, without complications.

## 7. Cord around the neck births

- Feeling uncomfortable around the neck region with clothing or other peoples' hands or apprehensive about any kind of physical movement around the throat area.
- Tendency to 'screen' or worry about everything before the event happens because it seems life threatening.
- May not want to fully participate in life because in some way it could 'kill' them.
- Could feel disconnected between their heart and their head and have difficulty expressing their feelings.
- Handle crisis well. The more threatening it seems to be, the more they want to prove they can live through it.

## Why choose to be a cord around the neck birth

- To be able to handle extremes and assimilate them with peace and ease.
- To trust you have a connection between your heart and your head that is open and rewarding.
- To sing your own praises because it is safe to speak up for yourself.
- To choose to make conscious choices about easing yourself into change with renewed life.
- To be passionate about loving deeply and feeling safe in showing it.
- To learn to continue to love going for life despite all invitations to do otherwise.

- To make change safe and do it with joy and ease.

## 8. Drugged births

- Tend to be lost in 'not knowing'.
- May feel their life is 'put on hold' while someone else's pain, fear, need, or life, is more important than theirs.
- Can have feelings of being cut off, going blank, a sense of 'nothing' or just a feeling of not wanting to participate.
- May feel cheated, incomplete and left out when not asked to be involved in an event because of another's control over it.
- Tend to be anxious about upcoming events because of their lack of confidence in not knowing enough.

**Why choose to be a drugged birth**

- To know where safety is and trust that you have a connection to it no matter how traumatic other's lives appear around you.
- To be fully awake to your own life and allow others to attend to their own needs without putting your life on hold.
- To be opting in rather than opting out when circumstances change or you are in the unknown.
- To learn to trust that being 'unconscious' because things are working is a safe place to be and be able to live with an open 'sixth sense' of things.
- To release the need to think you are missing something.

## 9. Easy births

- Tend to struggle in life or make things harder or more complicated than they are because of guilt of having it easy.
- Generally, find themselves not worthy or deserving of an easy life because they made the ease of their birth wrong.
- Because of their need for approval of others, they could go into agreement with the majority that if you are not struggling you are not alive, or if it is not done the hard way it is not an achievement.
- Generally, 'thru-time' people, planning ahead to have it easier later on. May have an over need to plan ahead for an easier life for fear of it getting harder later.

## Why choose to be an easy birth

- To give up the struggle and know there is an easier way than continuing to do it the hard way.
- To change the relationship with the past and end 'I have to struggle to survive'.
- To be here with ease, demonstrating an easy way of relating and being alive.
- To relinquish hardship as an idea, physically, emotionally, mentally and financially.
- To pick an advanced topic and ease your way through it.
- To release the pressure on others so they too can have it easy.

- To let go of any guilt in having it easy and know you are innocent in getting it right the first time.
- To know you can go through change easily and remember the bigger the change, the easier it is for you to handle.

## 10. Fast births

- Tendency to put pressure on themselves and others to get things done fast.
- May leave things to the last minute and need to rush to have them completed on time.
- Finding others are not ready for them because they have completed their task too fast.
- When conditions have changed to something unknown and uncertain, they may want to exit/escape/leave and get out of their fast to save themselves or another in some way.
- Could be really ready, yet when the event happens, it is so fast that they feel like they could be in danger.
- May have a tendency to hold themselves back if a situation seems to be going too fast.
- Could have a need to go over and over a task/conversation/ordeal to slow it down for fear of it being over too fast and as a result they may miss something.

### Why choose to be a fast birth

- To know that when you have a task to perform you can complete it quickly.

- To know how to leave a place quickly without labouring over staying too long at something that is over, or is not working.
- To achieve the goals you aim for, and attain them quickly.
- To have no blocks or nothing in your way to moving freely and easily in life.
- To excel at events/tasks that come easily to you because you grasp the concepts quickly and act on them without delay.
- To learn how to pace yourself as you grow and change through a task, accelerating at the appropriate time and then be able to slow down enough to receive the acknowledgement of a job well done!

## 11. Forceps delivered babies

- Often feel pressured in life.
- Find that when they really want to be going for it, they feel stuck or held back by situations and/or people, and need someone or something to pull them out, in order to free themselves of the pressure of it all.
- May 'explode' with anger and aggression because they are 'tanked' by whatever is happening.
- May continually live in the fear that somewhere pleasure will inevitably turn into pain and they will be worse off that how they began.
- May often feel they are under the pressure of someone else's authority.

### Why choose to be a forceps birth

- To know that you can handle anything that life asks of you.
- To go for it 100%, no matter what.
- To love, despite all invitations to do otherwise.
- To trust, even when it seems too painful to go through it.
- To learn ultimately that *pleasure leads to more pleasure* and not be held to ransom by life not working for you.
- To experience the tenacious drive to love deeply whatever the cost and to make this cost positive and prosperous!
- To know that you already know how to handle the pressures of being here.
- To enjoy the pleasure of being here and get on with the job of attracting those who can enjoy it with you!

## 12. Held back births

- Really wanting to be there, yet there always seems to be something holding them back.
- Wishing things would hurry up, yet something always seems to be in the way.
- Could feel held back because circumstances are not happening for them when they want them to.
- Need to break through the walls of resistance before they feel free enough to go forward.
- May not really want to get on with the job and use obstructions to get in their way.

- Have feelings of frustrations, bewilderment and confusion because they really want to get on with it and something is in the way.

**Why choose a held back birth**

- To have the determination and strong mindedness with where you choose to go.
- To know that no matter what is put in your way that has the potential to stop you from moving on in life and completing the task.
- To learn to live your life without struggle of something or someone in the way of your goals.
- To think about what freedom is rather than concentrating on what is holding you back.
- To know that being held back was not to keep you there indefinitely, it was to give you a little bit of extra time thinking and feeling about how to do things differently to achieve the end result…..freedom. and you did it!
- To realise that to make a bit of extra time on a task, or with a person, can be a blessing and easily achieved when you choose to see it differently.

## 13. Induced birth

- May be resentful towards others for invading their space.
- Could put themselves into fast forward, verbally or physically to see if they can work out a situation to regain control.

- May find themselves lacking in the get up and go that other's think they need to make a life.
- Tend to send out a message that they do not know how to get things started and thus need inducement from others.
- May let others decide for them, because they think they do not have what it takes to know their own way in life or what it takes to start a life.

**Why choose to be an induced birth**

- To learn how to become your own authority.
- To know how to use resources in the world to get started.
- To know that it is right for you to create what you need to bring about change.
- To handle change even though everything outside of you seems to be speeding up and out of control.
- To know how to turn others' help into positive change and move forward in your own authority.
- To offer others help because you are sure of your way, what you are doing and when you will be doing it.

## 14. Late births

- Will generally have people waiting for them to arrive, wondering what the delay has been?
- Tend to have people concerned about what is happening in their life.

- Physically may organise extra activities to do to delay being on time for an event, or being on time with completing a task.
- Could delay progressing through and event because they psychologically do not want to be there.
- Generally will want to tell you every detail of why they are late because *late* was/is so needed for their livelihood.

**Why choose a late birth**

- To enjoy the safety of not being confronted with what you do not know yet.
- To discover how to achieve many tasks in the time available, (and perhaps learn how to do less and have more time, and by doing less you may end up being early!).
- To learn to demonstrate your worth without the struggle or pressure of thinking you get it wrong by the outside world.
- To recognise your timelessness and know your timing *is* the right timing.

## 15. Near to death birth

- Tendency to pay attention to how a situation may 'die' away rather than enliven it.
- May feel like they are 'dying' because they are alive.
- Feel they are not recognised as worth living for.
- Attract people who tend to be concerned about their survival in life.

- Could demonstrate a need to stay separate from life, what it offers and the people in it.
- Could display a tendency to feel that their life is 'outside' themselves and that it is not really theirs.
- May have resentment of authority over them, because they have not learnt how to be fully alive themselves.

### Why choose to be a near death baby

- To 'wake up' and turn on to life and love being here.
- To get off feeling you need to 'die' again in order to live..... a key to having physical immortality.
- To reinforce that your life urge is stronger than your death urge.
- To understand that it could have been easier for you to die at birth rather than wanting to live and to know you stayed alive because you have what it takes to be here.
- To remember how resourceful and resilient you are in getting what you want out of life and to be able to give up punishing yourself and others for not being able to act from your strengths sooner.

## 16. Normal births

- Everything seems to go well, no complications, 'normal', yet they may feel that they are not important enough to warrant attention.

- Could feel that everyone expects them to handle everything like they normally do and therefore may want to do things 'out-of-the-normal' for a change.
- Could over strive for assistance rather than relying on themselves all the time.
- Tend to feel unsupported, alone, unassisted, with the feeling that they are not receiving the love they want.

## Why choose to be a normal birth

- To prove you did not need complications to be here.
- To know that whether or not anyone else is there for you, you have what it takes to naturally fill the criteria for performing the task put before you.
- To remember, if it becomes complicated, you have agreed to wrong thinking.
- To let go of thinking you have to change people's reality for you to be right.
- To learn to keep the connection to your faith and receive the love and support you need because it is working, not because you are reinforcing a weakness in you to attract attention.
- To remember that you did get it right, and you have got it together, and in the right way.
- To be patient in seeing who is able to support you as a success.

## 17. Premature births

- May have a tendency to move from a place, relationship or job 'prematurely' because conditions at the time seem to be too uncomfortable, or the pressure is too much, the noise is too great, the air too polluted, there is not enough food, or what is being digested around them is disturbing, negative and just too toxic to live in.
- When conditions are not the healthiest and their survival is being threatened, they will make the decision to help whomever is involved, to get through the experience quickly so they can 'get out of the condition early'.
- They have a strong will to live. They came here to survive so they will do what it takes to get the job done.
- Could fear being *too weak or too small* to perform tasks well. So they will tend to take on BIG projects, or tasks, and have themselves feel overwhelmed by it all.
- May organise others to pull away from them and keep their distance because they think themselves too much to handle and could be a burden to anyone who meets them.

### Why choose a premature birth

- To learn that *vulnerability is safe.*
- To take a big risk into the unknown and survive whatever it takes to grow and change.

- To be able to handle large amounts of attention, even though you could feel overwhelmed by it all.
- To be important enough to be 'nourished' and cared for when you are feeling at your weakest point in life.
- To be ahead of time putting yourself out there, compared to those you have collected around you.
- To see advantages in doing things early.
- To trust that everything and everyone is loving you, helping you and working for your highest ideal.
- To release the need to work *harder* than others' *just* to survive.

## 18. Turned at birth

- May feel that people want to turn them toward a direction that does not feel right for them.
- They are often determined that the way they are going is right for them and others seemingly want to impose their way upon them.
- Could find that their point of view is always different from that of their employer, partner, or family, and that they seem to always 'have to' relinquish 'their rightness' or 'their way of thinking' to fit into the life and lifestyle of others.
- May find themselves comfortable to be positioned in a life that seems right for them at the time and then develop a need to be turned, by another or others, in order to be more compatible in the relationship.

- Find themselves set up to fit into a position that is right for another and feel that its not right for them.

## Why choose to be a turned at birth baby

- To find an easier way.
- To remember that if life feels like a struggle, then you are going the wrong way.
- To be flexible and flowing and led in a direction where more life is an option.
- To learn that change is safe and that when you change, and let your life be turned around, you open up to something even better.
- To turn to the truth of what you are meant to be doing in order to be here.
- To transcend the need to want to change others so they do not change you and demonstrate how changeable you can be.
- To remember that you really want to be here and you did not do it by resisting what was there, you did it by 'resourcing' what was required to get what you wanted, a life.

# 19. Twins (multiple births)

- When growing and changing, could find themselves jostling for position with another (Twins) or others (Multiple Births).

- May feel in order to move forward in life they need to bring another, or others with them. Could always be looking for a play mate to feel at home in life.
- May conjure up ways to separate themselves from another in order to move on in life.
- Could find themselves wondering what position is in life. Are they required to lead, or need to follow someone else's lead?
- At times may feel comfortable sharing everything they have and at other times sharing may mean they could lose part of their own identity.
- Could feel financially obliged to help their significant other out of debt, or they could be willing to trade their beliefs to help the other out.

## Why choose to be born a twin

- To remember the value of being connected to love rather than fearing the loss of love.
- To reinforce a balance between leading and following, teaching and being taught, giving and allowing yourself to receive, being a planner and allowing things to be planned around you, to know and not know.
- If you have been too dominant in any area, to have the courage to play the other role for a while to learn why your Twin has been there, what the teaching is and take responsibility for your part.

- To know that true connection is never absent and that it does not always have to be a physical connection exclusively with one other (or two, depending on how many shared the womb space during pregnancy).
- To remember you chose to be here as a twin to learn to allow another to find their own way without needing to control it for them.
- To demonstrate being independent instead of needy.
- To remember that 'twinning' or 'soul-mating' is what we all thirst for, and you already have it fully developed. Love it rather than fear the loss of it.

## 20. Unwanted births

- May feel unwanted because they are not planned enough, not 'legal' enough, an accident, a mistake, or they are being left behind or left out of the experience or they feel a burden, physically as well as financially.
- Can often feel that 'something is not right' when they are around.
- May experience the fear of being unwanted as well as the fear of being wanted.
- They tend to be so confused about where they fit (in the family, in the job, in life), that they tend to have a big leaving pattern.
- Always looking for that elusive place of being wanted, constantly checking out the people, the places, the sports,

the jobs, you name it, to see where they are most approved of, loved and wanted.

## Why choose an unwanted birth

- To learn to be a welcome surprise.
- To love being wanted and accepted, and handle when you are not wanted.
- To know that not everyone wants you and what you have to offer. Let others be spread around and allow them to relate to others. Everyone is not for you.
- To hold yourself in high self-esteem for having performed the right activity in the right place at the right time, because things **had** to change.
- To realise, how courageous you are and the strength it took to be here. You are so wanted and very needed on the planet right now for holding change as a positive rewarding place to be. You have chosen it. Become it!

## 21. Wrong sex births

- Tend to have a strong need to be the right one and do the right thing for family and friends.
- Often feel under pressure not to be a disappointment by being wrong.
- Could be over achieving to get it right because of the fear of being found out that they are the wrong one.
- Find that the desire to be the right one, to look the part, to act the part, to live up to the expectations of others, is

a wearisome task and may have them struggling to know who they really are.
- In feeling that they are the wrong one and demonstrating behaviours that seem to be in opposition to the family's expected ideals and values, they will tend to be seen as living a life that is vastly different.

## Why choose a wrong sex birth

- To break the mould.
- To be unlike the others and be something different.
- To make your choice the ***right*** choice for ***you*** and learn to be a welcome surprise to your family, teachers and loved ones.
- To see there is rightness in everything and everyone, yourself included.
- To make the event more important than your fear of getting it wrong and let go of any doubt that you are the right one.
- To remember you are here because you are the right one. You are God's gift to the world and change is safe.
- To love being what is not expected. That is your talent. Embrace it! Enjoy it! You chose it because you have the strength and courage to live it.

*Robyn Fernance's book Being Born is available in digital format from:*
*https://www.breathandinspiration.com/robyn-fernance-being-born.html*

Were there some 'ah ha' moments of realisation as you read about the way you were born and the associated patterns and behaviours that were created from the combination of experiences at your birth? Some may be stronger than others. Some you may have already worked through and let go of. If you have children there may be some realisations about their birth. Using this information can be really helpful when trying to navigate being a parent. When children exhibit patterns of behaviour that appear to have no explanation as to where the behaviour came from this information may help understand and assist in managing the unwanted behaviour.

Robyn Fernance's book, Being Born also covers, how to work with each birth type, learning in the home and classroom, how to get along with others and how to relate better with each birth type.

We store fears, phobias, feelings, thoughts, urges and memories unacceptable or unpleasant, such as feelings of pain, anxiety and conflict in our unconscious. Once something that is in the unconscious is made conscious, it becomes easier to let go of. Understanding our birth patterns makes them conscious and allows them to be let go of more easily.

Something to think about, a female baby, before it is born has all the single cell embryonic eggs it will ever have. That means we are carried within our mother as a single cell egg, while she is in our grandmother's womb, before our mother is born. That means because cells carry memory, we can have cellular memory of trauma etc from our grandmother's life while she was pregnant and from our mother's life and her birth experience. All our incarnated lives are filled with layers and layers of known and unknown information gathered through experiences and we are here, in human form, to become conscious so we can let go of whatever prevents us from fully experiencing life in the moment, which is the only place we can truly experience love, peace and freedom.

Let's look at what we do when we are unable to cope with our mental thoughts and emotions attached to past traumas.

Robyn Fernance: Being Born, How your birth affects your learning performance, lifestyle and relationships. https://www.breathandinspiration.com/robyn-fernance-being-born.html

Chapter 7

# DRUG ADDICTION, DRUGS AND THE EMOTIONS THEY SUPPRESS

What is it we do when we are not coping in our life, when we have thoughts and emotions that we don't want to think or feel, often coming from an experience that has created trauma in our mental and emotional bodies and then gets stored in our physical body? We often use something to push the thoughts and emotions down because we are fearful that we won't cope or be able to deal with them if they come to the surface. We don't want to feel or deal with the negative emotions, because they are painful.

We as human beings are very good at not wanting to feel our feelings. We are often taught from a very young age (especially men) to keep our emotions and feelings to ourself, this causes the emotions and feelings that are not worked through and released to be stored in the cells of the body, eventually manifesting as disease. Any time we are confronted with a similar experience, the old memory that is stored, is triggered and we will do anything to suppress it, including taking drugs.

One of the reasons our parents (also siblings, friends and anyone we converse with) ignore or try to control the expression of our feelings is because when we are expressing our emotions, it can trigger whoever is listening. It can bring up their emotions that have been stored in their cells, from their own experiences, that they do not want resurfaced and to have to feel again. Our unreleased emotions come up because they have not been worked through and released from the original issue that caused them. If within a family, each generation is not allowed to feel their similar emotions, this can contribute to the same drug use that goes from generation to generation and the same diseases.

We often use drugs to suppress the negative emotions we attach to our negative thoughts (especially about ourself) that we do not want to feel. We suppress the negative feelings by getting 'high' on drugs. Each drug we use suppresses different emotions.

It is interesting how addictions can go from generation to generation. When I look deeper at this issue, I relate it to the way we take on similar thoughts and beliefs to our parents and siblings (both conscious and unconscious), which can translate into becoming habitual tendencies over time. If each generation, does not let go of the generational beliefs, we end up using the same drugs to continue to suppress the same generational thoughts and emotions that are not brought to the surface, faced and let go of. This I feel is contributed to by trauma from physical, emotional, mental and spiritual abuse (and also what we have made an experience mean, connected to our lessons that we have come into a human body to learn) that have not been resolved and released. Hence, I feel this is one of the reasons addictions run through families. If we choose our family as the perfect family for us to learn our lessons, then the drugs and addictions that are presented through our family, are our opportunity to work on our own lessons rather than lay blame on family members. After all we are responsible for what we drink, drop, smoke, snort and inject, no one holds us down and forces us to take it, no one does it to us, we do it to ourselves, we choose, even if it is unconsciously. Let's make it conscious.

It is interesting how we say drugs and alcohol, yet alcohol is a drug along with cigarettes, they are just legal drugs. I even see sugar as a drug. For many it is more addictive than cocaine and harder to stop taking.

Drugs take us (our consciousness, our soul) out of our body. We are in an altered state of consciousness and our self-awareness is depleted, we are in a drugged state, so we don't have to think our negative thoughts and feel our negative feelings, especially about ourself. The drugs supress our negative thoughts and feelings and they make us feel better about ourself, at least until the drug wears off. And there stands the problem, whereby a user prefers the illusionary feeling the drug gives them, to the real reality of how they feel when not taking the drug. Over time we become dependent and addicted to the drug to continue our false reality, supressing the thoughts and emotions we don't know how to deal with.

Let's have a look at what each drug may suppress.

The emotion that **alcohol** suppresses is FEAR. We drink to relax. If we think about what happens when we drink alcohol, we lose our inhibitions, our anxiety reduces and we seem to gain confidence. We talk and say things we would not say when we are sober. We do things we would not normally have the confidence to do and often after, regret what we did. Many accidents and injuries occur because someone has suppressed their fears and inhibitions and acted from that state, causing harm to themselves or worse to others.

Alcohol has an impact on the brain causing irreversible brain damage and cognitive function can be impaired, especially in those that have a heavy and long history of alcohol abuse. Alcohol is regarded as both a medical and social problem and one does not have to be labelled an alcoholic to cause both harm to themselves or others. Heavy and moderate drinkers, particularly binge drinkers, cause more harm in society and to themselves, as they often use alcohol as their excuse for their behaviour and actions, as if that was a good enough reason for the damage they have caused. No one gains from the destructive use of alcohol. The suppressed emotions of deep hurt often surface and are directed in an abusive way at partners and family members, especially innocent children.

The emotion that **Cigarettes** or nicotine suppress is ANGER. Smoking cigarettes is the drug of choice when a person has a lot of anger that they do not want to deal with. It makes us feel more relaxed reducing nervous tension, anxiety, anger, frustration, depression and fatigue that we may have been feeling before we light up, we feel we are more in control. When the level of nicotine drops in the body the person will feel the opposite, getting agitated and feel out of control, hence another cigarette is reached for and the addiction starts to form.

Nicotine affects the central nervous system, the more we smoke, the more we think we are relaxed. The truth is smoking makes it harder to breathe because of the tar that coats the lining of the sinuses, the bronchial tubes and the lungs, this in turn, suppresses feelings which usually flow in and out with the breath. This relaxed feeling is because the breath and emotions are being chemically suppressed so what we feel is deadened. Breath is life, so anything that inhibits it is detrimental to our whole being on all levels.

In BodyTalk, it is suggested that it is at the top and bottom of full breaths that the brain receives messages from the body that there is a problem needing to be addressed. If we (and particularly smokers) are not engaging in full deep breaths then the brain does not receive the messages of dis-stress from the body and can't do anything about repairing it.

The emotions that **Marijuana** suppresses is SADNESS and GRIEF. When someone is smoking marijuana, they seem to become happy and dopey hence the nick name for marijuana, dope. One of the main issues with smoking Marijuana is that at whatever age a person starts smoking the drug, their emotional body stays at that age, which means that emotionally they are usually very immature as they continue to age and have no self-realisation that this has happened. I personally find that clients who have been Marijuana smokers in their teens are less likely to manage their intimate relationships maturely. Clients that have smoked for many years seem to find it challenging to be able to look at themselves from an objective place because of the damage the drug has done to their cognitive development. If the use is heavy over time it leads to paranoid and delusional thinking.

The emotion **Heroin** suppresses is SELF-HATRED, the user loathes themself. Heroin is a very self-centred addiction, hence why those with an addiction to it have no issue using violence to steel or hurt another to feed their addiction. Heroin causes deterioration in psychological function and gradually undermines the ability to concentrate, leading eventually to memory loss.

The emotions **Cocaine** suppress are POWERLESSNESS, INFERIORITY and feelings of INSECURITY. The user takes the drug so they feel a greater sense of self-worth and self-assurance, giving them the feeling of being powerful. They become very talkative and think they are thinking very clearly and quickly, giving them the feeling of superiority, but in truth this kind of thinking results in the inability to assess situations clearly leading to paranoia, hallucinations, recklessness and obsessiveness. Because of the feelings of insecurity and inferiority that Cocaine suppresses, it makes it a very attractive drug to teenagers.

The effects of **Amphetamines** or '**Speed**' are similar to cocaine and the emotions cocaine supresses. The main difference being that the high lasts longer and is cheaper. On speed a user feels more self-confident, less self-critical, more daring and powerful. The thought process becomes less logical and conversations usually become two-dimensional and lack depth. Speed addicts have a tendency to pick at their skin.

The emotions **Ecstasy (MDMA, MethyleneDioxyMeth Amphetamine)** supress are ISOLATION, LONELINESS AND ABANDONMENT. Ecstasy reduces the fear that isolation, loneliness and abandonment produce and the user more easily expresses their feelings and this leads to feelings of wellbeing. As the user relaxes, they are unaware of the needs of their body ignoring signals that their body is needing to rest, cool down or hydrate. It can lead to destruction of muscle tissue and possible cardiac arrest. Mentally the user may become disorientated and hallucinate and have paranoid panic attacks.

Let's look at what some would refer to as lesser drugs or not drugs at all.

It is thought that **caffeine** supresses TIREDNESS, DESPAIR AND BOREDOM. It gives the brain the feeling of being more alert, which gives the drinker the illusion they are more alive and supresses the feelings of stress. Caffeine is found in tea and coffee, cola drinks and chocolate.

Socially, tea and coffee are used to help people communicate in a calm manner, they are like a social glue suppressing boredom.

Physical dependence, if a lot of caffeine is consumed can cause chronic insomnia, persistent anxiety and depression, stomach ulcers, infertility and long-term digestive diseases such as hypertension, osteoporosis and anaemia.

**Sugar** possibly supresses FEAR AND LOW SELF-WORTH. How many people have an addiction to sugar and find it very challenging to stop consuming it? Sugar, seems for many, to be very addictive and it is found (and hidden) in so much of the pre-packaged foods we consume daily. Alcohol and sugar are very similar biochemically, so the two, at times, may be used as a substitute for one another, suppressing feelings of low self-esteem and fear. If a person stops consuming alcohol, they may find their sugar intake increases to continue to suppress the emotions of fear and low self-worth.

**All addictions have their source in a spiritual desert. Meaning, instead of looking outside of ourself for answers we need to turn inward to find the answers, releasing blame externally and internally and choosing to take responsibility for ourself in our life. Once we let go of our internal critic, that little voice in our head that puts us down and replace our thoughts with kind, loving thoughts towards ourself, our outside world reflects our loving inner self, back at us. If we want more love, love ourselves more, if we want acceptance, have more acceptance for ourself.**

Drugs are a huge issue in our society. In this section I am only scratching the surface and recommend those that want to delve deeper into understanding the psychology of their addiction, where it comes from and how to work with the emotions they have suppressed and let go of them, to free themselves of their addiction, that they seek assistance with a professional. Working with clients with addiction and seeing the change they create in their life once they are free of their addiction is profound.

Much of this section has been drawn from Ruby Johnsons book, Your Drug or Your Life, Prescriptions for Getting Clear. Ruby with many years of experience both personally and professionally explores all the drugs I have covered in this chapter, plus other addictions such as Kleptomania, eating disorders, gambling, shopping, workaholism and co-dependence in her ground breaking book. I highly recommend sourcing a copy. Please refer to the appendix for details of where to purchase her book.

Chapter 8

# HOW WE LEARN THROUGH OPPOSITES

Have you noticed that everything has an opposite? Hot and the opposite cold, day and night, matter and spirit, positive and negative. Even emotions have opposites. We have the opportunity to learn through opposites. One of the ways we learn is through duality.

What do you think the opposite if love is? Most people say hate. I think it is fear. When we hate something, it is usually because deep down we are fearing something associated with it. I see fear, hate, anger and control as a vicious circle of negative emotion. Often when we fear something, it is because we are unable to control what is happening in the outside world, the situation we find ourself in and the outcome of our experiences with others. The strong emotion of hate and anger or both can surface and it stems from our fear of not having control.

Fear is a negative emotion, what other negative emotions and ways of being come under fear? Think about the negative thoughts the little voice in your head says and what feelings are attached to those thoughts and make a list. Here are some examples.

## FEAR.

| | | |
|---|---|---|
| Hate | Intolerant | Manic |
| Helpless | Impatience | Despair |
| Paralysed | Panic | Worry |
| Depressed | Guilty | Abused |
| Anxious | Unworthy | Rejected |
| Persecuted | Sad | Criticised |
| Jealous | Confusion | Muddled |
| Frustrated | Restless | Angry |

The list goes on, there are many negative emotions that we can feel if we are not thinking from a place of positivity.

What emotions and ways of being come under love? What loving emotions do you feel during your day and make a list?

## LOVE.

| | | |
|---|---|---|
| Acceptance | Freedom | Courage |
| Confidence | Trust | Enthusiasm |
| Caring | Compassion | Harmony |
| Contentment | Joy | Clarity |
| Peace | Bliss | Fulfillment |
| Calm | Happy | Creative |

And the most important one that most people forget, **self love.**

Which list do you spend most of your waking hours thinking and feeling from, the love list, the positive emotions or from the fear list the negative emotions? What percentage out of 100% of your thoughts and emotions are from the negative list and what percentage are from the positive list? Most clients when asked this question state between 70% to 90% in the negative column and 10% to 30% in the positive column. From which list would you like to spend your waking hours thinking and feeling, the love list or the fear list? The list that we think and feel from is up to us, no one else. No one can make us feel anything, it is what we make something mean, (often from old experiences being retriggered in the present experience) and what beliefs we have running, either front and centre or in the background, that create our thoughts and feelings.

If 'energy follows thought', what will happen if we keep thinking negative thoughts (and negative beliefs) and attach negative emotions to them? If we keep thinking negative thoughts and attach negative emotions then we will eventually manifest negative experiences into our life, including into our physical body as disease, become tired and not cope with life. How do we change what we are thinking and feeling? First, we need to become conscious and self-aware of our thoughts and our emotions, without consciousness and self-awareness nothing can change.

What do we have first an emotion or a thought? We usually have a thought first and then attach emotions to our thoughts. The emotions we attach are usually triggered from a previous experience that feels similar to the one we are presently in. We have memory of all of our experiences, both positive and negative stored in our cells as cellular memory, which can be triggered, at any time by a present experience and cause us to react, in a similar way, as we did in an old experience. If we have lots of negative thoughts and emotions, we will have a lot of negative cellular memory stored in the body.

The emotion of fear and many of the negative emotions are usually present either when we are thinking into our future or we do not want to re-experience something from our past, in the present moment or in our future. The old memory attached to the old experience triggers our emotional body.

We have to be conscious and self-aware of our thoughts and the emotions we attach to our thoughts, to be able to change them and let them go. Change is all about how conscious we are. We have to become more conscious of ourself, our thoughts and emotions. We can do this by remembering we are not our body, our emotions or our mental thoughts and step outside of ourself and watch, like we are watching a movie of ourself in our life. We can watch and listen to what we are thinking (and saying) and how we are thinking it and what the emotion is that we have attached to the words we are speaking and the thoughts we are thinking.

This is where the change can happen. This is the opportunity to let go of old limiting beliefs, old ways of being that no longer serve us, let go of the old emotions that we attach to the thoughts caused by the beliefs about ourself and about others. If we continue to have the same thoughts and emotions, we continue to have the same kind of experiences over and over again. For what reason would we do this? An opportunity to learn a life lesson is being presented to us through our experiences. By becoming conscious of ourself, in the experience, we have the opportunity to look at who we are being and what is triggering us. What is triggering us in the experience, is usually more to do with ourself than the other person. Remember our external world and those in it, are a mirror of our internal world, of how we treat ourself. By looking at our external world with consciousness and self-awareness, we have the opportunity to change it by looking at what it is trying to teach us about ourself and shift our way of being. Sometimes this is not easy to see, usually what we find we do not like in our outer world is what we are doing, thinking or feeling about ourself. Many people have no idea they are putting themselves down with their thoughts. We are often so hard on ourself, treating ourself disrespectfully with our internal dialogue, our inner critic, beating ourself up, over and over again. As we change who we are being towards ourself, the outside world changes what it is reflecting at us because we have learnt the lesson and it no longer needs to use duality as a mirror for us to learn, so we get to create a new possibility in our future.

Lessons are never ending some are big and some are small and each time we learn something about ourself and let go of an old belief and old ways of being that no longer serve us in a positive way, we move towards the positive emotions of love and self love and all emotions that enhance our life. I find most of the emotions in the love list we can only feel in the moment of now when we are conscious and self-aware, another great reason to live in the moment by being conscious and self-aware of our inner self and use the external world and the relationships we have, through observation, as our teacher.

Let's learn a technique to assist us to think and feel from the love list.

Chapter 9

# THE LITTLE VOICE TECHNIQUE AND THE BREATH

How does your mental body speak to you? Remember that little voice in our head from Chapter 1. What does it say? Does it say kind loving thoughts or does it criticise and put you down? Does it put others down so you can feel better about yourself? What does that little voice in your head say to you? What emotions do you then attach to those thoughts, remember we can't have a thought without an emotion?

When you try to stop it and shut it down, does it become quieter or get louder? What we resist usually persists.

Let's create a tool that can be used to change what we are thinking. It is called the little voice technique. Follow me....

Think of something that makes you feel angry.

Think of something that makes you excited.

Think of something that makes you feel sad.

Think of something that makes you feel enthusiastic.

How quickly could you think of each thought with the related emotion? Within a few seconds. What happened was, me, (coming through the words on the page) an external source, changed what you were thinking about and it probably only took a few seconds.

Were you thinking about anything else or just what I was asking you to think about, thinking of something, an experience, that had an emotion attached to the thought of anger, excitement, sadness and enthusiasm? This meant that the thoughts changed from a negative thought with a negative emotion attached, to a positive thought with a positive emotion attached. This is to show that we can change our thoughts from a negative to a positive quite easily, but it is interesting how much we can get stuck in a negative thought process, with a negative emotion and before we realise, it has been going on all day, often getting bigger and bigger and more and more negative the longer we think about it.

Let's work on changing our thoughts and the emotions we attach to our thoughts to be more positive and loving.

Remember we are not our mental thoughts we have a body of thoughts but we are not our thoughts because we know what we are thinking. We can hear our thoughts just like we did, when in Chapter 1 we thought our name and heard ourself think it.

Let's think of a negative thought, perhaps something that is constantly replaying in our thoughts about ourself.

Now say to the little voice that is saying that negative thought, "I hear you, thank you for sharing" (no resistance, only acknowledgement) and now notice how you are breathing.

Where are you breathing in the belly or in the chest? Do you have a longer pause after you breathe in or is it longer after you breathe out? Where is the longer pause in your breathing cycle? Do you have one?

While you were thinking of your breathing were you thinking of anything else? Usually the answer is no (a little more challenging when reading the instructions rather than hearing them verbally). What we are accomplishing, is by noticing our breathing, we brought ourselves back into the moment, away from the thought that was probably from our past or in our possible future.

How long do we have before we die if we are stopped from breathing? Probably only a few minutes. Breathing is the most important thing we do in our life, it is automatic, the body takes care of it, our body breathes us. Before I asked the questions about breathing, there was probably no consciousness about the breath, we take it for granted because our body breathes us. We have all been breathing while reading this book and given it no conscious thought. The only time the average person notices their breathing is if something happens to affect their ability to breathe, such as shortness of breath from exercising or an illness, smoking, something blocking our windpipe and choking us, an asthma attack or panic attack or being held under the water as examples.

Throughout our life we have many experiences. Our breathing is affected by our inability to release the negative thoughts and emotions from the experiences we have, especially those that are traumatic. We store unexpressed negative thoughts and emotions from our experiences in life, that we don't work through and release, energetically in our diaphragm. This, over time, affects our ability to breathe fully, as we breathe, is as we do life. Full breaths full life, shallow breaths, emotionally inhibited life. When the diaphragm is full, the negative energies are sent to our liver and our liver, being the organising organ of the body, sends them to different parts of the body, where they are stored in the cells as negative energy. The suppressed negative thoughts and emotions can be the start of disease in the cells of the physical body. It can range from stiffness and aches all the way up to diseases such as cancer, heart attacks, a stoke and autoimmune diseases.

The breath can be used very productively to remove thoughts, beliefs and emotional issues that are not serving our human experience in the form of breath work and also contribute in the BodyTalk process and other healing modalities. Meditation, Yoga, Qi Gong and Tai Chi or just sitting noticing the breath, which is a form of meditation, is healing for the physical body and calming for the mental and emotional bodies.

The breath can be used to bring us back into the moment. Many of our thoughts are either from our past or what we think are our possible futures. When we are criticising ourself, it is often connected to past experiences or what we think may or may not happen in our future. Deep conscious breaths, especially in the belly assist to calm the body and quiet the mind, keeping us more centred in the moment. We are concentrating on our breathing rather than letting the negative thoughts and emotions fill our mind. We are breathing our body consciously, in the present moment.

Once we have brought ourself back into the moment, after thanking our negative thoughts and consciously breathing, it is interesting to see how often the negative thoughts we were thinking have gone. We can now either stay in the moment, concentrating and thinking about what we are doing in that moment, whether it is driving, eating, working etc, or think of thoughts that are empowering and positive to create a life full of positivity and possibility, remember energy follows thought. What we think about in the moment creates our future, so if we are aware and conscious of our thought's we can create an amazing future. The only place we can find peace, freedom, bliss, harmony and all the wonderful positive, loving emotions are in the present moment. What we think in the present moment creates our future. What kind of future do you want to create?

There is no one born with our name, at the exact time we were born, with the same physical birth (birth patterns) and astrological configuration. This all contributes to our blueprint, making our blue print unique to us. This means we are completely original and unique, and that is amazing! So, let's tell ourselves how unique and amazing we are.

This technique is like flexing a muscle, the more we use it, the stronger it becomes and the easier it is to quieten the unruly, negative thoughts we think. What we think about now, in this moment can have a huge impact on what we create in our future. Negative thoughts, particularly about ourself, can create a future of negative experiences. Positive thoughts about ourself can create positive experiences, remember we create our life because we are the observer of our life. Because we are the observer and not our physical body, our emotions or our mental thoughts, we are, when conscious, able to choose with practice what we think. No one can think our thoughts for us, they are ours alone, we choose every one of them. Our physical, emotional and mental bodies make up our personality. As they become more balanced, through self-awareness and becoming more conscious our personality becomes more balanced and we can start operating at a higher level, allowing our soul to control our outer form and life and all events. This is the ultimate experience in a human body.

Each time we think a negative thought, catch the thought, say 'I hear you, thank you for sharing", come back to the breath, noticing how we are breathing and once centred in the moment with the breath, think kind, mindful and positive thoughts about ourself and others. Remember we are all unique and amazing.

Chapter 10

# WE LIKE TO BE RIGHT

Who likes to be right? We all do, no one wants to be wrong it is a natural behaviour to want to be right, even if it is mostly in our thought process and not outwardly expressed.

Who knows they are right about people and how they will act or behave or what they will say, especially parents, siblings, partners and our children?

Did you know that for us to be right a person must show up how we believe they are going to show up? If we believe and see them as selfish, they must show up that way for us to be right. If we believe they are argumentative they must show up that way for us to be right. If we believe they are controlling, they must show up that way for us to be right. If they show up any other way, other than how we **expect** them to be, how we **believe** them to be (our belief about them) then we would be wrong.

We even look for evidence and/or agreement, both consciously and unconsciously, that we are right about what we believe about a person or situation based on our beliefs about them or the situation. We can look for that evidence through the next experience we share with them or by getting others to agree with us about the persons negative behaviour. We attract in people and experiences that show us the evidence that we are right, based on our conscious and unconscious beliefs, especially about ourselves. I think we set up experiences to prove we are right about them. We create experiences to test them to see if they can pass the text and when they fail, we have more proof they are what we think of them. Remember as the 'observer' of our life we create our external world and the experiences we have. As an example, if we have a belief that our partner is controlling, we will find ourselves experiencing them as controlling. If we have a belief that we are not listened to, we will attract in people who interrupt us or talk over us or ignore what we say. Many of our beliefs are established from our birth process, our lessons we are here to learn (our birth timing astrologically and numerologically) and through our parental experiences as children and teenagers. Over time we will find the evidence showing up of what we believe, to show us we are right about how others treat us. For what reason would we do this?

There can be several reasons why we do this. Remembering that others are mirroring back our lessons for our growth and development, (as we are also doing for them) so if we have a lesson to learn we will have beliefs, usually negative, about ourself and others associated with our experiences that we create to learn our lessons. We have beliefs about everything, thousands of them, especially about ourself. Are they really true, look at the words believe and belief they both contain the word 'lie' within them, be-**lie**-ve and be-**lie**-f? Most of our beliefs and what we believe are lies we have made up or been brainwashed to think are real. The negative beliefs we have about others, are usually more about how we feel about ourself. This is how the reflection of what we think (believe) about ourself, both positive and negative comes back at us via those in our external environment. Let's look closer.

Pick someone close to you that you have an issue with, using mother, father, sibling or partner is best, and write down how you see them. How do they show up? Are they intolerant, bossy, always telling you what to do, untidy, unkind, aggressive verbally, emotionally or physically, emotionally unavailable, critical, how are they being that you don't like? Perhaps they let people walk all over them and don't stand up for themselves or do everything for everybody and never put themselves first.

Now write down how you would like them to be, how they would be behaving if they were having the best life for themselves (not for you). Write it in the positive not in the negative. As an example, the positive would be, they take time for themselves or they put themselves first or they take care of their health by looking after their physical body and they are healthy. Perhaps they would have great self-worth and treat themselves with respect, mentally, emotionally and physically. They may be open and good communicators, or have a great sense of humour and be very social, calm and gentle. Perhaps they would be emotionally available to talk with depth and understanding. Write down the way they would be, (for them) to have and enjoy a fabulous life with positive behaviour, not what we want them to be for ourself.

Now let's look at the first way, the negative way that we saw the person and take time to look at the behaviours we don't like and become aware of each behaviour. It is not usually something we want to see. Look closer, do you treat yourself the way you are seeing this person? Do you bully yourself with negative comments, from your inner critic, that little voice that never shuts up? Do you become intolerant towards yourself, when you do or get something wrong? Do you criticise yourself over and over again, beating yourself up with your own thoughts and emotions? Do you get angry and frustrated with yourself when you don't achieve and compare yourself to others? Are you unkind to yourself? Do you physically abuse yourself with drugs (including alcohol and cigarettes), food, lack of sleep, lack of exercise, the list can be very long?

Now if we notice what we have written about the other person and look deeply at ourselves we will probably see, (if we look consciously) what we do not like in that person is what we struggle with and how we disrespect ourselves. We may even see that we treat others in a similar way, but it is more likely that we see how we inwardly mistreat ourself. It is the mirror, the reflection, so we can see what it is we consciously need to change about how we treat ourselves. Those external to us, particularly our family members, will not stop reflecting our lessons at us until we learn them. When we are kind, mindful and treat ourself with love and respect, others can reflect back at us the same kindness, mindfulness, love and respect. Sometimes when we get the lesson, if the person is no longer needed for the lesson, they may move out of our life, especially when our lesson is related to our self-worth.

Now look at the list of attributes you wrote down for the person to have the best life and ask yourself, do I need more of this in my life? As examples, do I need to be kind and accept myself just as I am (stop the inner critic), do I need to be emotionally available (to myself), do I need to put myself first and be calm and communicate to myself what my needs and wants are?

Many a time when I ask my clients to do this process, the reflection of what they do not like in another, is how they mistreat themselves and the behaviour that would give the other person a great life, is what they need to be and bring into their own life. The external world is nearly always a mirror for our growth and learning.

Let's look a little deeper at the beliefs and how they affect our life.

Chapter 11

# HOW WE ATTACH EMOTIONS TO OUR MENTAL THOUGHTS TRIGGERED BY OUR PAST

We are unable to have a mental thought without attaching an emotion to that thought. We are unable to feel an emotion without attaching a mental thought, they go together and here lays the challenge, especially when the thoughts and emotions are negative.

We have a choice about the thoughts we think and the emotions we attach to those thoughts, so what is the reason that so many times we think negative thoughts and attach negative emotion to our thoughts?

Each experience we have is a new experience, so what is the reason that we often react negatively in that new experience, repeating the same behaviour and emotional reactions similar to other past experiences we have had? Where does the negative thoughts and emotions in the current experience usually come from? It often comes from a past experience, that is being triggered by the present experience because they appear similar.

When we have an experience that feels similar to a past experience, the emotions and beliefs (mental thoughts) attached to the old experience get triggered and we relive them through the new experience and react in a similar way, which is often an inappropriate reaction to the present situation. Usually, we are not conscious this is what is happening as our physical, emotional and mental bodies go into autopilot and we lose control and say and do things, often not understanding the reasons behind our behaviour. Instead of being able to respond calmly and with appropriate levels of emotion we react, sometimes defensively, or angrily, sometimes completely irrationally. It can feel like we become the victim of the experience, if that is our pattern.

Every cell in our body holds memory. If we have had an experience (including the in utero and birth experience) and not worked through the trauma and made it conscious, the feelings and thoughts attached to that experience, that are negative or traumatic, will be stored as pathological consciousness in our cells. This includes our organs, endocrine system, heart, brain, blood, joints, every physical part of our body (this can include our Etheric body our Chakras and Meridians). When we have an experience that triggers our beliefs, emotions or past trauma, the cellular memory is triggered and the body goes into fight or flight mode and all the associated emotions, thoughts and physical responses are triggered and reoccur.

Each time we have an experience, (especially when we were young), we create beliefs about ourself, about others and about our environment. The beliefs come from the thoughts and emotions that we made up during and after we had the experience. I use the words 'made up' because many times what was actually experienced and what we made it mean are very different. We are meaning making machines, our mind is always adding our own reality to an experience, often because of past trauma and unresolved negative patterns. Hence why two people can have a completely different view of another person or of something they witnessed or both experienced. Remember we like to be right, so we see each experience through our own set of beliefs and patterns, especially the negative beliefs we have created. We create our experiences from beliefs and negative patterns of behaviour that are intrinsic to the lessons that we chose to work through before we came into a human body, for our growth and evolution. It is our job to make them conscious and let them go, replacing them with positive patterns of behaviour and in the process uncovering our gifts and talents that the negative behaviours have hidden.

How can we change or let go of our negative reactions? Therapy helps!!!

When we are more conscious of ourself, separating ourself from our physical, emotional and mental bodies, we can take our awareness to view ourself and our reactions, instead of making it about the other person and allow ourself to feel the emotions that are attached to the thoughts and see if we can find a past experience where we felt that same emotions. The first experience we remember is often found back in our childhood. The unconscious cellular memory that has instigated the negative behaviour in our childhood is often further back, in the in utero and birth experience. Remembering that our parents (and siblings) are unconsciously behaving in ways that show us our lessons, so we see who we are being and what we need to change, or let go of that does not serve us, for our self-development and personal growth, moving ever closer to fully loving and accepting ourself.

Who is in every relationship we have? We are. We are the only person that is in every relationship we have, so how can it always be the other person.

When we use our new realisations that there is an unlearnt lesson now showing up in this present experience, it tells us we have some unfinished business with ourself (not the person who is reflecting at us the opportunity to learn). We can look inward to search for the original experience and the emotions and thoughts attached to that experience. What is the unlearnt lesson that is now being mirrored back at you, for you to have the opportunity to learn about yourself? How are you treating yourself? Do you have healthy boundaries and limits with yourself? Do you know how to say no? It could be any number of beliefs that are stopping us from living our best life and need to be changed or let go of? They are not always easy to find but it can be extremely rewarding when we see our lesson and let go of an old pattern that does not serve us in a positive way. Once the lesson is learnt the mirroring stops, we no longer need to attract in experiences for the lesson. We can tick another one off our list and move on to the next one.

Can we ever make a mistake, can we ever get life wrong?

## Chapter 12

# MISTAKES

Can we ever make a mistake? I don't think so. I think we make mis-takes. Let me explain.

Remember when I said we are not our physical, emotional and mental bodies and when conscious we can separate ourself from our bodies, watching ourselves think our thoughts, feel our emotions and watch and feel our physical body. This makes us the observer of our life which means our life is like a movie we can watch when conscious and self-aware.

Now when making a movie, each scene is repeated, until the scene is the way the producer wants it. Many takes may be done to get the scene exactly as it needs to be, within the context of the whole movie. Take 1, take 2, take 3, as many repeated performances of the same scene are done until it is perfected. This is an analogy of our life. We don't make mistakes we are practising, until we learn the lesson the scene (our experience) is teaching us. We create many mis-takes in our life, we can't make a mistake, it is impossible, because life unfolds in perfect order, even when it appears chaotic and painful. We are unable to see how each mis-take effects the big picture of our life. Often, we have experiences that are related to a potential future experience that we have no idea or concept of. Like in a movie an early scene in the movie is setting up for future scenes, that as yet, we are unable to see, until we get to that part of the movie. We have to have trust that there is a bigger picture we are not privy to because our learning comes in the not knowing, as well as in the knowing.

It is creating an opportunity for each of us, within our own life, to be gentle with ourself when we make a mis-take, remembering we are practicing trying to master being a human being and if we had it all sorted and perfected, we would not need to be in a body to grow and evolve ourself. Each mis-take is the gift for us to go within and accept ourself just as we are, loving ourself through the process of learning, so we can come out the other side, closer to who and what we really are.

Can we look at our beliefs (and thoughts) and renegotiate with ourself without having to have experiences mirror back at us the same lesson? Let's look a little deeper.

# Chapter 13

# SUPPLY AND DEMAND

There is always someone to supply what we consciously or unconsciously demand, as proof, we are what we think we are, especially our negative critical thoughts about ourself.

If we think a certain way, such as 'I am clumsy', 'I am stupid', 'I am unattractive', 'I never get it right', 'I can't make friends', 'people don't like me', any number of negative thoughts about ourself, there will be someone to supply us with the evidence that we are what we think we are. How much does your inner critic, the little voice that is critical towards yourself, have to say about you?

Remember because we like to be right, if we think we are a certain way and listen to that inner critic, then what we think will be reflected back at us from the outside world and the people in it, so we have the evidence that we are right.

Because of our need to be right we demand, often unconsciously that someone, (usually more than one, sometimes many) will supply us with what we demand. The stronger the belief is, the more proof will be supplied that we are what we believe ourself to be.

Energy follows thought. What we think creates our reality. What we think will be supplied to us in our outer world and mirrored back at us, after all we have asked for it as evidence that we are what we think we are. Would you like that to be a positive experience or a negative one?

In relooking at who we are, we get the opportunity to renegotiate what is supplied to us from our external world. In changing what we believe (and think) about ourself we get to have a new supply of incoming proof.

As we look inward and renegotiate with ourselves who we are and realise our full creative potential and unique and amazing qualities, we can create positive, kind, mindful and harmless thoughts and beliefs about ourself. This changes our external mirror of what is reflected back at us from the people we have relationships with. The supply of what we think and feel about ourself from our outer world, that we demand unconsciously for evidence that we are right, can now be shifted to a more positive state, mirroring back kindness, mindfulness and harmlessness, more love and peace because we are now aligned with positive loving thoughts about ourself. This serves our growth towards loving and accepting ourself and others. What a wonderful world we could have, if we all aligned with positive thoughts of love towards ourselves. It would mean, what we demanded consciously for us to be right, would be supplied to us by those that are in our external environment. The love reflected back at us would be the evidence we are right about our love for self and others.

Chapter 14

# DEPRESSION, ANXIETY AND THE MOMENT

Do you suffer with anxiety? Who feels they get depressed? Who feels they get both anxious and depressed? How do you get there? What are you thinking about and feeling when you are anxious or depressed?

Let's look at depression.

Often when someone is feeling depressed their thoughts are about the past, 'If only I hadn't lost my job', 'if only my partner had not left', 'if only my mother had been kinder and not so critical', 'if only I did not get this disease'. The negative thoughts can be about how we feel about ourself, our external world or the people in it and are usually associated with past events and past experiences and the stories we make up that we attach to those experiences. Over time, the stories can grow and become more depressing and bring up deep negative feelings about ourself and the situations we experienced in the past. We can be triggered by past experiences, when we have a present experience that brings up similar thoughts and emotions to the old experience or trauma. We often recreate similar experiences throughout our life that activate the triggers from our behavioural patterns that become cemented in our childhood. We have our own interpretation of what happened and what we made the experience mean, often attaching negative thoughts and emotions to the experience. There can be a lot of blame, usually at those that were a part of the past experience. Could there be an opportunity to learn a lesson from that past experience?

With these types of thoughts from the past, a person often becomes very self-critical in the present. 'If only I did not have that scar, I would be prettier', 'If only my mother had not given me sugary sweets, I would now be thinner', 'if only that hadn't happened, I would now be in a better place'. It is endless what we say to ourself. The inner critic, that little voice in our head, saying lots of negative thoughts and then our emotional body attaches negative feelings to the thoughts. It is often repeated over and over again, the thoughts become more depressing along with the feelings we feel.

With depression we are mostly looking back into our past experiences and memories and wishing they were different, often blaming them for our present situation. We are wanting our life to change. Often, the opportunity is being presented so we can look inward to see the past experience differently from a new perspective, from an internal perspective, with the opportunity to clear some negative thoughts and beliefs about ourself.

When we don't like ourself (depression can be associated with self-hatred that is turned in on one's self) we often isolate ourselves from others and this makes the depression worse as we feel unsupported and all alone. It can also be that a person is surrounded by people and still they feel all alone in their depressed state. We live in a world of technology that has the effect of isolating us even more because we no longer need to be in another's physical company to communicate, which usually means we create more thoughts in our head because we spend more time alone and do not have an outlet to let them out of our mental and emotional body and work through them. I believe this is creating more depression in our society.

Let's look at anxiety. When suffering anxiety, we are often thinking, 'What if someone breaks in?' 'What if he leaves me?' 'What if she dies?' 'What if I lose my job'. 'What if I don't lose weight?' Lots of what if's!

With anxiety we are often thinking about something that we think may happen in our future, we convince ourself that it is going to happen and we can spiral into a panic attack, creating shallow breathing or if really bad, stop breathing all together. We start filling our mind with thoughts of impending disasters. We create a fear of the future by what we think and believe may happen or not happen in our future. We have thoughts and beliefs that are negative and then attach emotions to those thought's that are also negative, about something that has not yet happened, and spend a considerable amount of time worrying about it. While a person is in the state of anxiety, it is very challenging to see any way out and they spiral into a more negative state, often adding more scenarios to the future they cannot live in, as it has not happened yet.

The fear of not having control of what we 'think' may happen in our future, that we are imagining, creates the anxiety we feel. The fear of having no control of our future, which contributes to the anxiety, is often associated with old experiences where we felt we had no control and the experience was traumatic and we don't want to repeat it, hence the anxiety surfaces. Plus, as with depression our lessons will keep presenting themselves via our experiences throughout our life, until we learn them.

Where is the only place we can live? Can we live in the past? No. Can we live in the future? No. We can only live in the present moment. It is amazing how much time most people spend thinking about their past and/or their future and how little time we actually spend in the present moment. How many times have you driven somewhere and not remembered parts of the journey or how you got there because you have been so far out of your body or in a trance state while driving? How many times have you been doing something and injured yourself because you have not been in the present moment concentrating on the task at hand? How many times have you been with your partner and not remembered the experience or conversation you shared with them? Even during the sexual act of making love most are not present to their partner or their own body and all the feelings that are available to experience because their mind is somewhere else. What can we do to get ourself back in the present moment?

Using the Little voice technique, we can take ourselves out of the past and out of the future and into the present moment and ask ourself, "Am I safe?" "Am I safe right now?" The answer is usually yes, if we look around at our environment, where we physically are, nothing is actually harming us, physically, mentally or emotionally. (If the answer is 'no I am not safe', then please remove yourself from the situation as soon as possible.) It is our thoughts and emotions of our past experiences and fears of the future, that take us out of the moment that we are in and when this happens, it can feel like we are not in control. The truth is, we are never really in control, there is a bigger picture (THE PLAN) we have no idea about that is going on behind the scenes. Yet we fear losing control and lose trust in the perfection of life and all the possibilities that we have in any moment. Trusting that life is unfolding perfectly even with all its dramas and that 'it too shall pass'.

I have noticed that fear is usually associated with the future, the unknown, rather than the past. Sometimes it is the fear of repeating the past in our future that causes our anxiety, so it is still associated with the future.

Using the breath consciously to bring us back into the moment, (the little voice technique) can help take us out of the depression (thinking of the past) and anxiety (thinking of the future) and bring us back to the now, which is the only place we can truly live. Here is where we can consciously take ourselves out (remember we are not our body, emotions or mental thoughts) and watch ourself, the thoughts the mind is thinking and the emotions the emotional body is feeling, like we are watching a movie of ourself and bring in new awareness and consciousness that is positive, from a place of self love, that is kind, mindful and harmless to ourself. We miss out on so much that is available in the present moment physically, emotionally, mentally and spiritually, when we spend the moment of 'now' thinking of the past or future. If we want to experience peace, the only place we can is in the present moment. If we want to experience freedom, it can only truly be experienced in the present moment. It is the same for bliss, harmony, joy, contentment, fulfillment, acceptance of ourself and all positive emotions. When we fully accept ourselves exactly how we are, love and respect ourself in each moment, we have the opportunity to experience all the wonderful feelings, that I sense, most people are wanting to feel, all of the time. This is what is possible in the present moment, which is the only place we are able to truly experience the art of living.

Our past has made us who we are now. Everything we have experienced in our past has sculptured and moulded us into the human being we are in this present moment, along with the behaviours and patterns that we are here to let go of and those that we have already released. The more we let go of what no longer serves us, our negative behaviours of self-destruction, the closer we get to who and what we really are, giving ourselves the opportunity to 'be' the love we are and create full acceptance of our human journey, with all the experiences, (that appear either negative or positive) that we create to further our evolution.

Lessons still unlearnt and still being experienced are all a part of who we are right now. The lessons being reflected back at us, through our relationships and our environment, are waiting for the opportunity to show us our inner negative patterns and behaviours, the ones that we direct at ourself, that we still need to let go of.

When working with a client that suffers with anxiety or depression, I bring to their attention how powerful our thoughts are and the words we put out into the world. If we think and say to ourself and to others, that we are anxious or depressed we are telling ourself, through our thoughts and words, that that is what we are. The words depression and anxiety are used so much in our society, especially around mental health. Now when people call themselves depressed or anxious the listener often attaches a very negative view, as does the person saying they are depressed or anxious. What if we replaced the words anxiety and depression with the word pressure? How is a diamond created, by pressure? How does a pressure cooker cook a wonderful meal, it uses pressure? Pressure is force upon something and that force has the ability to create change. (The word 'depression' means low in spirits, the word 'pression' means act of pressure.) When we are feeling depressed or anxious, we are applying force on ourselves by what we think and feel. The pressure we create on ourselves is an opportunity to go within and let go of what is causing the pressure, the thoughts and emotions that are from our past or what we think may happen in our future. Instead of using the words depression and anxiety, replace them with the word pressure. As an example, when someone asked how you are feeling, a reply could be, "I am feeling under pressure at the moment by the circumstances I am dealing with".

Because what we think (and then often say out into the world) is so important let's look at some words that can contribute to negative feelings.

The word 'should' or 'shouldn't' can creates guilt, adding to anxiety or depression. It feels like it leaves us no choice. As examples "I should lose weight" or 'I shouldn't eat that', or 'I should help my family'. What if we replaced the word should with could? Now we have choice. Look at our examples, "I could lose weight' or 'I could choose to eat that' or 'I could help my family'. We now have choice and we can choose freely whether we do or whether we don't. We need to think with our heart to make choices and feel with our head, acting for our own highest good because if we do something out of guilt, the energy behind what we do is negative and that is what we store within ourself and put out into the world. Incorporate the word 'would' by asking ourself the question, "What would I do in this situation if I was loving myself and acting for my highest good"? Be empowered by the words we use, using 'could' and 'would' and no more 'should' or 'shouldn't when thinking or expressing outwardly to others, creates choice and power instead of guild, anxiety and depression.

Here is another example how we stop ourselves from having choice by the words we use. The words decide, suicide, genocide, homicide all are made up with 'cide' which means to kill or cut off and 'cision' (as in decision means to cut). When we decide something, we are killing off or cutting off other possibilities. Instead think 'What would I like to choose?' Make choices, choose what outcome is best and if after new information is known or circumstances change be free to choose differently. So often we corner ourself into situations where we feel we have no freedom to change our mind because we 'decided' or made a decision.

Remember, words whether thought or spoken can have a powerful effect on us, think from the heart and use them wisely.

Changing what we think of ourselves and the words we speak can assist us to shift ourself to a more positive, empowering state.

Chapter 15

# VEHICLE VERSUS VEHICLE

Who has a car? Do you service your car regularly when the mechanic tells you to, every so many kilometres, even though there is nothing wrong with it? Do you insure it? Do you clean it? Do you drive it with bald tyres or replace them when they need replacing? Do you put good fuel in the car? How much do you think you spend on your car over the life of the vehicle keeping it in mint condition? How often do you replace your car? Do you replace it when there is nothing really wrong with it, perhaps because there is a new model out or you just want a different car? Do you have more than one car?

How long would you like to live, give me a number, an age you would like to live to, 80, 90 perhaps 100 years? How many more years would you like to be on the planet and in what condition would you like your body to be in, especially when older? What kind of fuel do you put in your body? Do you put sugar and junk food in your body or good healthy food like organic fruit and veg? What about liquids, fluorinated tap water and soft drinks or clean pure filtered water and fresh juices? Do you put drugs in your body? Cigarettes, alcohol, Marijuana and other chemical drugs, perhaps lots of coffee and caffeine etc. What about on your body, chemicals in makeup and skin care products, or chemicals from the kind of work you do? What thoughts do you think about yourself and others positive, loving and kind or negative, unkind and abusive?

Do you service your body, even when there appears to be nothing wrong with it, like you do with your car? Do you get it massaged, take it for walks and exercise it, keep it fit and flexible, meditate to relax and connect and take it into nature to recharge and rejuvenate it? Or do you just wait till it breaks down and then want it fixed and repaired?

How much money do you invest in your body, the vehicle that you do life in, to maintain it and keep it healthy and in good working order?

It is interesting how much we spend on a car which we replace every so many years and yet we neglect our body, the very vehicle that has to last us for the whole of our life, from birth to death. If our physical vehicle is unwell or diseased, we may not even be able to get in our car, our second vehicle, the one we drive around in (our physical vehicle is our number one vehicle) or be capable of driving it because of poor eye sight or dementia or the body physically may be incapable of standing to walk to the car. We can't replace our body. We may be able to replace some parts such as a hip or knee but would you rather not go through that painful expensive process?

Do you want to have a body that is aged beyond its years or would you prefer a body that is younger than its years?

Our body is the vehicle we do our life in, yet many treat it with so much disrespect. When we do not care for our mental and emotional bodies, keeping them positive and letting go of negativity, the end result is usually a physical body that breaks down and becomes diseased and worn out before its time. Working through and dealing with our mental thoughts and emotions is really important for our physical body.

A big part of a healthy body is self-love, if we loved ourself, we would treat our body as the holy temple that it is. We would care for it by putting healthy food in it, the good fuel. We would be careful what we put on it, using products free of harmful chemicals to both ourselves and the planet. We would keep it fit by regularly exercising it. We would do things to maintain it rather than waiting for it to break down, using massage, yoga, meditation, sun shine, walks in nature, lots of clean water and taking time to rest it, so it can rejuvenate.

All our bodies, physical, emotional and mental are connected (making up our personality) and balancing them is very important for each of them to stay healthy and in good working order. The next time thoughts go to replacing the car with a new model, check in to see if the number one vehicle, the physical body, is needing any servicing and personal care and attend to it first, so it is in the best of health for as long as possible. Living with a positive, balanced mind and calm, peaceful emotions, helps to create a strong, resilient and healthy physical body. The condition of our temple, our body, reveals how balanced our emotional and mental bodies are and how much we love ourself and our life.

Chapter 16

# DISEASE AND HOW WE MAKE OURSELF SICK

Disease, let's look at the word. Let's break it up, dis-ease means we are not at-ease. When we are at-ease, we are in a positive state. The opposite way of being is dis-ease, we are in a negative state this is how we often manifest dis-ease. Dis-ease and at-ease are a form of duality.

Remember in chapter one, we talked about what Quantum Physicists have discovered, that everything in the universe is made out of energy, including us. They discovered that physical atoms are made up of vortices of energy that are constantly spinning and vibrating, each one radiating its own unique energy signature. In observing ourselves this means we are beings of energy, vibration and we have a frequency. The composition of an atom under a microscope shows a small, invisible tornado-like vortex, with a number of infinitely small energy vortices called quarks and photons and as we focus closer and closer on the structure of the atom, we would see nothing, we would observe a physical void. The atom has no physical structure, we have no physical structure, physical things really don't have any physical structure. Atoms are made out of invisible energy, not tangible matter.

> Nothing is solid & Everything is Energy – Scientists Explain The World of Quantum Physics: by Conscious reminder off the internet

If we are energy and energy follow's thought, then what we think about will manifest into our physical body. We become what we think. We attract and or create what we think about, on both an unconscious and conscious level. If we ask ourself, are my thoughts positive about myself or does my mind run riot with negative thoughts about myself, and others and the world I live in?

Remember, we can't feel an emotion without having a thought and we can't have a thought, without attaching an emotion to that thought. If we are constantly having negative thoughts and emotions from our life experiences and from our relationships and not working through the lessons that they are here to teach us, stuffing down the unpleasant emotions with food or drugs, (including alcohol and cigarettes) we can eventually manifest a dis-ease in the physical body. My experience is that people who are very negative, particularly about themselves, often have low energy, tire easily and get sick often and people with a positive outlook, are more energetic and have high levels of energy. Our cells need positivity to stay healthy. If they are not fed with positivity, over time they can become dis-eased from all the negative thoughts and emotions.

There are a number of books that have been written that explain and give the negative mental thoughts and emotions that can contribute to each dis-ease. Some have the positive thoughts that would contribute to the healing of the disease. I find the shift from external blame to the internal realisation that we create our life and are responsible for what happens in it, plus the letting go of the inner critic and other positive conscious shifts, greatly contribute to a person's improved health and wellbeing. It is interesting when I read out the negative thoughts and emotions that are the cause of the dis-ease my client is suffering, how many times they agree that it is what they are thinking and feeling or suppressing in the case of feelings. I will list the books I use in Appendix.

We often don't realise what we are feeling, we have buried trauma from experiences throughout our life and we lock down the feelings and emotions with drugs or food or shopping or any number of addictions. Sometimes we just stop engaging in life and either have very few relationships or in extreme cases, none, so we don't have to feel the old pain, from our past, reflected through our present relationships and experiences. Sometimes we hold on to relationships that are toxic and keep reliving our trauma through others, blaming others rather than looking at ourself.

Many of our thoughts and emotions become unconscious, as we lose touch with ourself, not wanting to feel our inner pain, but they do not go away until we face them, make them conscious and work through them, coming out the other side with a lesson learnt.

There is a lot of science related to dis-ease and how positive and negative thoughts effect our physical body. Scientists who have an interest in energies, are studying what happens to our cells when we think certain thoughts and feel certain emotions and the effect that has on the brain and the cells of the body, like stress. As an example, we are about 83% water and water has been proven to have memory and is affected by the negativity or positivity of its environment. Dr. Masaru Emoto, the Japanese scientist (who wrote the book The Hidden Messages in Water) who revolutionised the idea that our thoughts and intentions impact the physical realm, especially water, tells us that we are affected by what we think and feel. On my water purifier and water bottles I have written positive words such as self-love, love, harmony, calm, joy, peace and freedom to create a positive effect on the water.

Often it is what we make something mean that has been said to us (or even just a look), which in reality is not what was meant, we are meaning making machines, always finding a meaning behind everything and it is often just a story we make up. We do this with our relationships with people all the time. How can two or more children growing up in the same house hold, witnessing the same experiences, have such different memories. We each come in with different ways of being, with different lessons to learn and are at different places in our evolution, so our interpretation of events is affected by our personal filters which are unique to each of us.

As we go through life, we start forming beliefs about ourselves and others, often negative or detached from reality, we make them up due to experiences we have gone through and the beliefs appear real. We attach old experiences to new experiences bringing the old emotion and mental thoughts to the new experience. Over time the negative beliefs, thoughts and emotions that we feel, affect the cells and the energy systems of the body, including our meridians. We then have the potential to manifest dis-ease in the physical body. This continues until we learn what the original experience was trying to teach us. This contributes to how we create our dis-ease. When we remove old memory and pathological consciousness from the cells of the body, we can have a positive effect on the dis-ease that we have created. I have had many clients who have healed or improved their dis-ease by changing their thoughts and emotions in a positive way and incorporated energy work into their self-recovery. I also give thought to the strong possibility that many of my client's future health is changed for the positive because they have let go of old limiting beliefs and ways of being that could have created dis-ease in their future.

It takes a lot more energy to think or hold down a negative thought, rather than a positive one. It depletes the body, stresses the cells and affects the physical body making it tired, weak and open to infection and dis-ease. Most of the mental thought and emotion that contributes to this is not from our external world but from our own inner critic, our little voice about how we think of ourself, related to our interaction with the outside world and the relationships we have. This is why, how we think and feel about ourself, is so important to our wellbeing, every negative thought contributes to the dis-eases we create. All the positive thoughts keep us at-ease and healthier.

How do you want to think? What do you want to feel? What kind of health do you want to have? If we can make ourselves sick and dis-eased by our negative thoughts, then we have the opportunity to reverse our dis-ease or stay free of it, by thinking and feeling from a positive state. The more positive talk we have for ourself, generally the more energy we have and the healthier we are. We all can contribute to our own wellbeing by thinking and feeling from a place of love, acceptance and respect for ourself and others. Be mindful, kind and harmless with our thoughts and emotions, especially when it is about ourself. Interestingly our internal positive way of being creates the same in our external environment, which means we have a direct impact on those we have relationships with, humanity and the planet. Never underestimate the power of love and loving.

Chapter 17

# DEATH, DYING AND DIS-EASE

Many people fear getting sick because they associate it with the possibility of dying. What if I suggested that we never die, instead we change form, after all science has determined we are energy and energy can't be destroyed.

I see dis-ease as an opportunity to delve deeper within to learn about ourself, our negative beliefs, how we talk to and treat ourself and let go of what does not serve our best self. After all, most dis-ease we create by how we live, think and feel. We have the opportunity to heal ourself from many dis-eases.

If energy can't be destroyed and we are energy, then at the death of our physical body, our energy body must retract and continue its journey back to source. Do you know how to retract your energy body at the time of death of your physical body? I don't know how to do this and I have yet to have a client or friend that does either. I have heard that those that are much more advanced at a soul level, can at will, leave their physical body. Highly advanced monks and those that have many years and experiences in the world of esotericism and meditation have this ability. Because we are not able to leave our body at will or know the appropriate time to pass out of physical form, we often become unwell with a dis-ease that will eventually cause our physical death. It is inevitable that each of us will at some point leave the planet. What this means is that most people will create a dis-ease that is to end their life.

I have worked with clients who were very sick, some would call them terminally ill, yet they have healed their life, their relationships and themselves before they left their physical body. At any point we have opportunity to heal and grow and evolve. The resolve of someone being able to die in peace with a sense of freedom because they have gone within and become conscious and self-aware and cleared their slate so to speak, is humbling and a privilege to be a part of.

The fear of death is often present when we have no faith in knowing we are all connected to each other, that energetically we are all one and all return energetically to the same place, source, when we leave our physical body, our vehicle, that we do life in while we are here. Trusting in the process of life, knowing that our physical death is a part of a much bigger picture that most are not aware of at this point in our evolution, can alleviate a lot of anxiety and allow us to be present in the moment where all life is meant to be lived.

Chapter 18

# DETACHMENT

What is detachment? How do we learn detachment and for what reason would we want to be detached?

What happens when we are attached to an outcome? It can create anxiety. The anxiety, can become even stronger, when we are attached to an outcome that is dependent on another's behaviour or actions.

If we are attached to a plan of everything being a certain way, leading us to an end result, which we have perceived as the outcome we want, we will generally find the outcome we get, does not measure up to our preconceived, expected outcome. When we have an experience, either personally or involving others, and we have attachment to a predetermined outcome we are expecting from that experience, we are not living in the moment, we are living in a future that does not exist yet. It is the attachment to the outcome that is the issue. Very rarely does a preconceived outcome become our reality, especially when it involves others, it may be similar but rarely the same due to our distorted view of life, our inability to control others and our wonderful imagination. This can lead to disappointment because of our attachment to what we want the end result to be. It is healthy to think positively about the outcome, just not be attached to it, instead care deeply from an objective place.

What control do we have over another, none! When we have an attachment to an outcome, we are often trying to control others so we get the outcome we desire. We need to relinquish the sense of authority we have over another and also of responsibility for each other's activities, and while doing this be able to stand shoulder to shoulder working together, whether it be within the family or a work place.

Our point of view and consciousness is ours and ours alone and right for us, to presume it is right for someone else is not coming from a live and let live way of being or a love and let live way of being.

What may seem clear to us and of vital importance to ourselves, may not be of the same value or importance to another.

Relinquish the tendency to criticise and adjust another's way of being, such as their work, the way they bring up their children or how they dress or present themselves. How many parents continually criticise their children, both consciously and unconsciously and don't let the child learn by their own experience. Many times, the criticism is covert, it is hidden, but the criticism is there. As an example, when children ask to put up the Christmas tree and they put the ornaments and tinsel on and it may be lopsided, have no order or look messy, it may not be how the parent envisioned the tree, not the outcome the parent is wanting. When the children have gone to bed the parents rearrange the ornaments and tinsel because they want it to look a certain way when friends and family come to the house. The parents make it about themselves and they have an attachment to how the tree is meant to look. When the children see that the tree is not the way they decorated it, they often feel they did it wrong or it was not good enough and they take it as a criticism, they can internalise it. Their decorating and creativity, has been corrected. The children's decorating skills are that of a child not of an adult. A kinder approach, is to leave the Christmas tree exactly as they have decorated it and when guests arrive point to the tree and show the guests what a wonderful job the children did of decorating it, the guest are now aware, that the way the tree is decorated, is the masterpiece of creative children.

We need to relinquish the responsibility for the actions of others, making sure our own actions and activities are up to standard, that is our responsibility.

We need to relinquish the pride of mind that thinks our way is the best or only way, that it is the truth and correct and that another's is wrong or false.

## Detachment is caring deeply from an objective view

Trusting that each situation or experience is exactly how it is meant to be in that moment, without judgement, leads us to a sense of freedom and peace. It is easier to stay in the moment, enjoying the experience, rather than getting ahead of our self when we attach to the outcome.

Detachment is viewing experiences and observing them without an attachment to the outcome. In each experience, whoever is present, are exactly the right people. Timing is perfect, when an experience begins it is always the right time. Whatever happens in the experience, is perfect and is all that could happen, no more, no less. When the experience has ended, it has ended perfectly.

# Chapter 19

# CAN'T GIVE FROM AN EMPTY CUP

If you imagine a cup and that cup represents you and its fullness represents how much energy, good health, positive self-talk, self-care and self-love you have for yourself, how full is the cup at present?

How full is your cup with good energy, love, compassion, great self-worth, personal power, quality alone time to rejuvenate, self-nurturing and the ability to give and receive equally?

If your cup has only a small amount of all of these necessary ways of being in it to live a healthy, happy and love filled life, how can you give to someone else if you do not have it and what is it you are giving them instead? We end up giving others, particularly those closest to us, the dregs in the bottom of the cup. It is interesting how often we give more to a friend or even a stranger than we give to our parents or partner and even sometimes our children.

When you say yes to someone but you really want to say no, what do you feel, what thoughts do you have? If you feel obligated to give or give to get something back, how do you feel? What kind of thoughts fill your mind when you are giving to another?

When we give from an empty cup, we usually end up feeling depleted and resentful towards the people we are giving to. Our physical bodies, minds and emotions are often drained and exhausted.

What are some of the reasons we can't say no and continue to give? Sometimes the person has not even asked us for our help but we give anyway and then resent them for not appreciating the help we gave them.

Some of us give to get approval from others. Some give so they can find a place where they feel like they belong. Some give because their culture says it is expected. Some give because they watched their mother give to everyone except herself. Some give so they feel good about themselves. Some give so they can control an outcome.

Many lessons that we are here to learn show up via our ability, or lack of it, to give and receive in a balanced way. If someone is always giving, they may be here to learn independence or self-awareness of their own needs, perhaps moderation in how much they give. The lesson may be about working on their self-worth, awareness of their personal values, awareness of boundaries, honouring their own needs first or strengthening their will power. It may be to raise their self-confidence or ability to love themselves and approve of themselves, without giving themselves away. What do you notice about all of the possible lessons? They are about working on one's self, not on working on others or our relationships with others, it is about working on the relationship we have with ourself, which in turn will change our external relationships. Who is in every relationship we have? We are in every relationship we have. We are in every one of them, so how can it always be the other person? If our relationships with parents, sibling and partners are not going well, we need to change our focus inward. As we change ourselves and get a different perspective on who we are being in our relationships and what our lessons are, our internal shift means once the lesson is learnt there is no need for it to be projected back at us by another person. So many times, when a client has shifted who they are being inwardly within their relationship with themselves, their external relationships take on a whole new dynamic and are healthier.

If our cup is not filled with self-love then we have very little true love to give. If our cup is not filled with compassion and kindness to ourself first, then we have very little true compassion or kindness to give. If we do not love and respect ourself, know our worth and what we are worthy of, then we are unable to receive from others. The relationships we have will reflect back at us what we lack, hence no one may give to us and we will have an inability to receive.

When our cup is full, we can give without depleting ourselves and what we give is of value to another.

We need to fill up our own cup with kindness to ourself, lots of healthy energy, self-love and self-care. We need to be conscious, of when we need to fill up our cup and when it is inappropriate to give, when our cup is depleted.

We need to fill up our own cup first, so we can give from our heart and receive back into our heart.

True giving, true service comes from love without an expectation of anything being returned.

We need a full cup that is overflowing with positive self-care and self-love, so we can out flow, the over flow to others, without depleting ourself in the process, creating healthy giving and healthy receiving.

Chapter 20

# THE BEAKER AND CHANGE

How challenging can it be to change our way of being, to let go and try something new. We want to change but the unknown can be scary so we stay as we are, instead of stretching outside of our comfort zone and taking a chance.

When we are stuck in life, it feels like we are standing in mud up to our knees, we can't move, we have no direction. We don't want what we previously had or what we have now but we don't know how to move forward into something new. We usually don't know what we want, so we are unable to move forward.

Let's use the analogy of a glass beaker, (like we would have used at school in the science lab) and we are standing inside the beaker, with our nose just above the rim and the stuck feeling, we are experiencing, is thick mud we are standing in up to our knees. We are unable to move, the mud is so thick. The mud represents our limiting beliefs and our negative thoughts and feelings about ourself and those around us, that prevent us from having a wonderful life. The beaker represents the environment we live in.

If we do not make changes to our inner self, our outer world generally does not change. When we look inward and make changes to ourself and who we are being, letting go of limiting beliefs about ourself, our external world changes. This changes our perspective on who we are in the world. When we improve our perspective, by becoming more conscious and self-aware, we start to have new ways of seeing ourself in the world. This new information and new perspective, is like fresh clear water pouring into the beaker. With the new information, we create new ideas and new directions that we want to explore, plus new insights and our relationships start to change. We have improved how conscious we are and raised our self-awareness, this is the fresh water now filling up the beaker we are standing in, diluting the thick mud.

As we change our inner self and the new information comes in, (fresh water pouring into the beaker) the old beliefs start to get diluted, (the mud) but until the new ones are second nature and we build muscle by repeating healthy new behaviours, it can feel like we are drowning. It is like we are in no man's land, old habits and behaviours are going and the new behaviours are taking their place but have not become a habit yet.

The great thing is, when we choose our lessons to learn before we take on our body, we only choose lessons that we have the capability to achieve, even if at times it feels like we are drowning, we don't give ourselves more than we can handle. We are stronger and more resilient than we realise, especially if we are able to accept change in our life.

As the water starts to overflow out of the beaker, taking the mud with it, the water starts to clear, the new healthy ways of being becomes second nature, we feel better and more stable. We have to trust that even when our life feels like it is drowning us, there is always the opportunity to clear out the mud and bring in new fresh water and a renewed sense of self. How many times do we give up just before the break through is within reach? Pushing through, so we can come out the other side, with new learnings is so worth our effort. Trusting the process, with its perfect timing, we are always in the right place, at the right time, doing the right thing, even if we feel like we are drowning. It too shall pass, when we look inward and shift who we are being and how we feel about ourself, to a positive state of loving kindness and harmlessness.

Let's look at what can happen when we change how we see ourself and let go of old ways of being even if only in a small way.

Chapter 21

# A SMALL INTERNAL CHANGE CAN CREATE A BIG EXTERNAL RESULT

We often want our external world and our relationships to change, so we can feel better about ourself. We think if something or someone in our external world changes, we will be happier. 'If everyone approves of me, I will feel better about myself'. 'If I have the perfect partner, I will feel complete'. 'If I can control my external world then I will feel in control and it will be safe to be myself'. 'If everyone would acknowledge that I am right, I would feel understood and accepted'. 'If others would recognise my contribution, I can feel good about myself'. Our external environment and our relationships are our greatest teachers. They create the opportunity to learn about ourself and assists us to uncover who we truly are.

As life reflects at us our lessons, it is showing us what we need to let go of, in order to be our true self. We do not have to become someone else by adding to ourself, we are being asked to let go of who we are not, so our true self can be expressed, from within, out into the world. By doing this we change our direction.

Everything in our external world, including our relationships, are being created by us, for us to see who we truly are on the internal plane, so we can let go of the patterns of behaviour that prevent us from living an extraordinary life. Each time we make an inner change we shift direction and our external environment will change because of our internal shift.

While we push against our external environment and the relationships we have, blaming them for what is happening in our life, expecting them to change, we miss the opportunity to create powerful and extraordinary outcomes.

Each time we consciously shift our thoughts towards self-awareness, using positive reinforcement mentally and emotionally, creating inner change, we get to create the possibility of a new external experience and new relationships that work. A small shift in how we see ourself and those we have relationships with, can create a very different direction in our life.

When a client starts to make the internal shift, becoming more conscious and self-aware of their inner thoughts and emotions, particularly towards themselves and then see the external result and how quickly that result occurred, often after one session, they are keen to keep the flow going to create more, of what seems to be external changes but is really the effect of their internal shifts.

If everything external to ourself is a mirror of our internal world let's look at how we can create someone who treats us badly by our thoughts.

## Chapter 22

# BULLIES AND THOSE THAT THEY BULLY

Bullying is an ongoing and deliberate misuse of power in relationships through repeated verbal, physical and/or social behaviour that intends to cause physical, social and/or psychological harm. It can involve an individual or a group misusing their power, or perceived power, over one or more persons who feel unable to stop it from happening.

Bullying can happen in person or online, via various digital platforms and devices and it can be obvious (overt) or hidden (covert). Bullying behaviour is repeated, or has the potential to be repeated, over time (for example, through sharing of digital records).

Bullying of any form or for any reason can have immediate, medium and long-term effects on those involved, including bystanders. Single incidents and conflict or fight's between equals, whether in person or online, are not defined as bullying.

Bullying has three main features:

It involves a misuse of power in a relationship, it is ongoing and repeated, and it involves behaviours that can cause harm. The above information was taken from the bullying no way government website. https://bullyingnoway.gov.au/WhatIsBullying/DefinitionOfBullying

Is it the bully that is the problem? Or is it the person being bullied? Let's explore.

It sounds a strange thing to say, is the person being bullied the problem? How does a bully act? They are generally very critical, make nasty comments and abusive, including verbal abuse, emotional abuse and physical abuse, and sometimes spiritual abuse.

What kind of people generally get bullied? Does someone who is really confident get bullied? If our external environment reflects back at us our lessons what is the bully reflecting at us? Where do we criticise, make nasty comments and put downs, where do we abuse, verbally, emotionally and physically? If you are someone who gets bullied, you may say I don't, I am not like that, I don't do that to others.

Now let's look at how we generally treat ourself. We say unkind and harmful comments to ourself, it's our own inner critic, the little voice that is often on repeat, saying negative and critical comments, over and over again. Think about how many negative or unkind thoughts the mental body tells us daily, compared to how many positive uplifting thoughts it produces, just in one day, and imagine over time how many negative comments are thought in a week, a month, in a year or a lifetime. The amount will be staggering.

We have so many children and teenagers (and adults) who have an inner critic, that inner voice, that is so critical towards themselves. We often abuse ourself with our inner voice, we attach negative emotions to the thoughts we have about ourself. The more we think negatively about ourself, the stronger the negative emotional reaction becomes, it can be extremely debilitating, causing depression and anxiety. Because of the way we think and feel about ourself, we turn on our physical body and physically abuse ourself with dieting or over eating, lack of exercise, self-harm, alcohol, cigarettes and other drugs. We are the biggest bully to ourself and so the person bullying us is reflecting back at us the way we treat ourself. The way we think about ourself, when negative, is so disempowering. Long before a bully turns up to reflect back at us our inner negative thoughts, we usually have been criticising ourself for a long time prior to them appearing in our life.

Let's look again at the three main features of bullying. It involves a misuse of power in a relationship, it is ongoing and repeated, and it involves behaviours that can cause harm.

Let's break this down. Feature one, bullying involves a misuse of power in a relationship. The first relationship we have is the one with ourself. When we treat ourself with disrespect and put ourself down, using negative thoughts and attaching negative emotions to those thoughts, we are creating a misuse of power in the relationship we have with ourself. Our relationship with ourself is the most important relationship we will ever be in. The longest relationship we have is the one we have with ourself.

Feature two, it is ongoing and repeated. Do we usually stop at one negative comment, no we repeat many negative thoughts about ourself over and over again, day after day, week after week, month after month and often year after year?

Feature three, it involves behaviours that cause harm. Every time we say something or do something to ourself that is negative, we are chipping away at our self-worth, we are prematurely aging and negatively affecting the cells in our body. We are not at ease if we are harming ourself with negative actions, thoughts and emotions and can create dis-ease. We are our own worst bully.

If we are hard on ourself and bully ourself, we will attract in as a reflection the same, someone being hard on us, someone who will bully us. We abuse ourself through inner criticism, so we attract in the same as the reflection, the mirror, from the environment and those in it. We are the bully, to ourself, first.

What is the lesson? Stop the inner criticism, stop the physical, emotional and mental abuse that we do to ourselves constantly. Be self-aware and conscious of what we are thinking about ourself.

What is the opposite to the inner critic? It is being kind to ourself, with our thoughts about ourself. I often ask client's, who is the person they love the most (the response is often their children)? I then suggest that the advice and comments they would give and say to the person they love, they need to use for themselves, until they can gain enough self-awareness and consciousness to give themselves positive advice. Let our inner voice be full of loving, kind, harmless thoughts, that we would normally give to the person we loved the most in our life, until the person in our life we love the most, is ourself.

The skill is to learn to be mindful of our inner conversations and aware of our emotions and mental thoughts. Practice harmlessness towards ourself, only kind, mindful and harmless inner comments are allowed. What someone else thinks of us is none of our business. It is more about them than it is about us because we are reflecting at them their lessons.

Imagine then, what the bully has going on within themselves. We do what we see, not what we are told. Often a bully has been abused, verbally, emotionally and mentally and repeats the pattern, they generally also have low self-worth and cover it up by bullying others and do not want to get in touch with their inner self. They are often very sensitive and are unable to deal with their sensitivity so in the process they become insensitive and hurt and abuse others. Some have a lot of self-hatred and they spit it out onto those they abuse. If a child is repeatedly told they are useless, stupid, dump, worthless or will never amount to anything, any number of negative ways of being, they can become what they are told because their own mental body continues with the abusive thoughts (the inner critic). On the surface, they may seem self-confident but this is the mask they wear to cover up their overly sensitive nature, that is deeply hidden, under the outward insensitivity that is projected onto others. The victims of the bullies are also usually very sensitive.

Here is the reflection back at the bully. They are just displaying their sensitivity differently.

The bullies lesson is to get in touch with their deeper true self, the sensitive part of themselves, that they have hidden because of their fear of being hurt, (so they hurt first) and instead, allow themselves to be vulnerable and in their true feelings. This can be a challenging lesson.

On the surface the bully and the person being bullied may look like they are complete opposites but when we dig deeper into the subconscious, we find a lot of similar emotions and pain within their psyche.

We learn our lessons through duality, opposites, so the bully is unconsciously giving the person, that is being bullied, the opportunity to change who they are being internally, how they treat themselves and to find their personal power, courage and strength and learn to love themselves. The victim of the bully, is reflecting back to the bully, the lesson of being sensitive and vulnerable and for the bully to be able to find a safe place to feel and express their emotional and mental pain. I have worked with a number of people, both students and adults, that have been bullied and each time when they change their inner critic to an inner voice of kindness and compassion towards themselves which lifts their self-worth, their whole external world changes and becomes a much more positive reflection and the bullying stops.

The more we love ourself, just the way we are, the more we are in our personal power, the less likely we are to be powered over. The stronger a person's inner resolve is, the less likely they are to become a target of someone powering over them. We are energy, our energy comes from our thoughts so the more positive our thoughts are, the more positive is our energy and the higher is our vibration and frequency and that is what another person feels energetically. We feel each other's energy, both consciously and unconsciously, so if a person's energy and vibration is low, they can become an easy target to be bullied. Their frequency will match the low frequency of the bully. Raising our energy with self-love, knowing who we are and standing in our personal power makes us energetically strong.

Be courageous to shine, be courageous to stand out, be courageous to trust we have everything we need within us. After all we are all unique and amazing. When we shift the inner critic out of our head and replace it with empowering thoughts, we thrive.

Let's look at a visual tool that we can use to show the effect of bullying.

Chapter 23

# VERBAL ABUSE AND BULLYING

Take a piece of new A4 paper (or something similar). Now let's listen to our inner voice and the thoughts we have about ourself. Think about, how we feel about ourself, the things we tell ourself that we are, or aren't every day. What does our inner voice say to us, I am too fat, I need to lose weight, I am stupid I can't even get a simple thing right, I am useless, I feel so lazy, I am not pretty enough, I hate my bad skin, I don't like my face (or parts of it), I never get things right, I am not as good or as pretty as my friends, I am not a good mother/father, wife or husband, I am a failure in the eyes of self or parents, and any number of similar comments. (If at this point you are feeling better about yourself after reading this book, use the old behaviour of negatives thoughts to do this exercise). As we are thinking these negative thoughts about ourself, I want us to take it out on the paper. With each thought, feel the emotion that the thought produces and show what that feeling feels like, the effect it has on the piece of paper. It may end up scrunched, torn or screwed up into a ball, whatever negative emotion we are feeling about ourself, take it out on the paper.

Once we have got all the negative thoughts out and taken them out on the piece of paper, I now want us all to put the piece of paper back how it was when we first took it in our hands. How are we going with that, is the paper back to how it was when we took it in our hands, no creases, smooth, no rips and only one piece? I would say the answer is no. It is impossible to return the piece of paper to its former state. It is never the same again. It is now in a new state, perhaps it has creases all over it. Perhaps it is in a few pieces or maybe in many pieces. It is permanently damaged.

Each time we mentally and emotional abuse ourself with our inner voice, (our little voice) we damage our own energy system, we weaken our cells and we can even cause them to turn on each other, just like we are doing to ourself with our negative thoughts. Luckily the damage we do to ourselves, with our negative thoughts and emotions, can be stopped by us at any time if we choose to change our inner voice to think kindly, lovingly and accept ourself, just as we are, in each moment. When do you want to start that process? Now is the only moment we can be in, so now is the only time to start changing and reversing our mental thoughts towards ourself, by thinking loving, kind and harmless thoughts about ourself and of course include others as well.

Each time harmful thoughts and words are projected towards another person they too have a negative effect, because energy follows thoughts and we are energy. It negatively effects those that think or speak the negative thoughts and words as well as those that they are projected onto.

The more they are said and repeated, usually the greater the effect on ourself and the other person. Remember what we give out eventually comes back to us.

When we, as a parent or grandparent, husband or wife, sibling or relative, teacher, student or friend, think or say negative, harmful, unkind words we too represent the destructive force of the hands destroying the piece of paper. Is that who you want to be in the world?

Each time we think and speak negatively, either to ourself or to another, we erode a little more self-worth, a little more self-confidence and self-love and it is replaced with a little more self-doubt, a little more unworthiness, feelings of rejection, feelings of abandonment, feelings of helplessness, feelings of alienation, fear and guilt.

The spiral begins, often taking someone into depression or anxiety, wanting to repress feelings of sadness and anger, fear and worthlessness.

What most people are unaware of is that, what we think or say about another person is what we inwardly feel about ourselves, we need to become conscious and self-aware to change this. It is the mirror, the reflection of ourself, the parts of ourself we do not accept or like, that we need to change that we see in the other person.

Look at our hand when we are pointing at someone, telling them off, how many fingers are pointing to the other person and how many are pointing back at ourself. Usually, one finger points away from us and three are pointed back at ourself. Who is it really about? Whether we point our finger or say the thoughts or only think them it makes no difference, it all has the same effect and is more about us than the other person.

When we have self-love for ourself, when we are kind and mindful with what we say and think about ourself and treat ourself from the position of mindfulness, kindness and harmlessness, then we have no desire to put another person down, we would only want to build them up. Other people, particularly our parents, partners and siblings are our greatest teachers to show us our lessons of how to do this, whether it is showing up as what not to do, or a quality to be copied.

# Chapter 24

# THE DESTRUCTIVENESS OF EXTERNAL COMPETITION

What happens when we compete outside of ourself? What happens when we compare ourself and try to be like someone else or be better than them? We are usually competing to feel better about ourself.

How often, when we compete, do we truly feel better about ourself and how often do we feel worse than before we started to compete and compare ourself to someone else?

External competition comes in many forms. Sports, academia, at school, in the work place, with our bodies, how we look, what we wear, social media, money, prestige, occupation, success, family and relationships and friendships, love and approval the list goes on.

How do you compete and what does it cost you personally when you do?

When we compete outside of ourself we very rarely win, there seems to be someone faster, smarter, richer, more successful, more popular, prettier, has a better body, has more friends, knows the right answer and the list goes on.

What is external competition trying to teach us? What is the lesson?

When working with a client, I point out to them that they are unique because no one was born at the exact time they were born, with the same name they chose for themselves (their date of birth and name creates their individual numerological make up), with the same birth conditions that were present at their birth (birth patterns), with the same position in the family and who look like them physically. It is interesting in the animal kingdom, what I notice, is all tigers look the same, they may have a slightly different coat pattern but basically, they are almost identical. It is the same with elephants, dolphins, insects and most wild animals. Domestic animals who have a slightly higher level of consciousness than other animals do look more individual. Dogs for example have many different features. In the human race almost everybody looks different, their hair type and colour, combined with their facial features, eye colour, body shape and size, skin colour and voice are so different. Yet people seem to want to look like, be like, behave like and have what others have. It is our consciousness that sets us apart. If we are unique and there is no one identical to us on the planet, how can we compare or compete with someone else? We are so individual. We are meant to look different and have our own unique way of being, we each have our own set of unique skills, knowledge and experiences. We have chosen (before we come into our body) what we need, in all forms, to learn our lessons while living our life. We choose the perfect body, the prefect family and the perfect experiences, in the perfect environment, (even though sometimes we wish we had chosen differently, all is perfect as a reflection for our learning) so we can pass the tests we give ourselves to grow and develop, while moving through our life experiences as a human BEing.

We can never repeat an experience, each one is different and no one can have the same experience twice. Another person can't have or see our experience the same way we do because their reality is different, which makes competing with another, within an experience, a waste of time and energy. We can choose to have a different and better experience than the last one, constantly looking to improve ourself, for ourself and enjoy each individual experience, without competing with another.

The only competing that truly serves us is to compete with ourself to work towards balancing our mental, emotional and physical bodies, which make up our personality. Balance is the key. Improving our skills and abilities to better ourself, assists us to find balance. We do this with our ability to be conscious and self-aware.

The only person we can truly compete with is ourself, through self-improvement, being kind and accepting of where we are and what we have in every moment. We are always in the right place, at the right time, doing the right thing, giving ourself the opportunity to love ourself a little more, just the way we are.

Self-acceptance and loving ourself exactly as we are, in each moment, with the knowledge that our desire to be better than the previous moment, pushes us forward to grow and evolve ourself, as we move towards mastering the human experience.

Chapter 25

# WHAT SOMEONE ELSE THINKS OF US IS NONE OF OUR BUSINESS

We often worry about what others think of us. Do they approve of what we are wearing, how we look, the size and shape of our body, what job we have, what car we drive or house we live in, who we have as friends, if we are married or single, what our culture or nationality is, how we speak, what we say, what we do or don't do and most of all who we are being?

If our external environment is a mirror of our internal environment, (how we think and feel about ourself, including all of our beliefs), then who are the thoughts and judgements really about?

What another person thinks of us is usually what they think and feel about themselves, although generally they are unaware of the reflection, it is unconscious. This means that what they think of us is really none of our business because their interpretation, thoughts and judgements of us, is their reflection of themselves. It is their opportunity to work on their lessons (we have to be aware and conscious to be able to do this).

It is the same for ourself, what we think of another person is none of their business as it is usually about ourself. It is our reflection, usually of an unlearnt lesson, resurfacing, being mirrored back at us, as an opportunity to learn something about ourself.

Many of my clients will express to me that people in their lives, often family members and partners, treat them the same or appear to be the same kind of person. This happens because, until the lesson is learnt, it will keep reappearing in those that are closest to us, especially unlearnt lessons with a parent showing up through a partner.

We can only see in another, what we have going on in ourselves. It is the reflection of behaviour that we generally do not see in ourself, (until it is made conscious) and it is usually the reflection of how we mistreat ourself, rather than how we treat or mistreat another person. Unless we are consciously working on our way of being and our lessons, we are generally unaware of the lesson that lies under the other persons behaviour, for us to learn about ourself.

Taking on board what another person thinks of us can have a negative effect. It generally is not about us.

Do we ever really know another person? What another person thinks of us is their reality not ours, it is more about them than us.

Imagine being neutral about what others thinks of you and how freeing that could be. Not taking on their opinion and their issues and being able to smile and walk away. If we use self-awareness, when we think and speak negative words to another person, we are able to consciously look within ourself about what we are about to say and check in to see who is it really about, them or us? We have to be in the moment and conscious to do this. This is an excellent way of changing the relationship we have with ourself, which in turn changes the relationship we have with others. As we continue to build our love, approval and acceptance of ourself, we will find we have fewer negative thoughts and comments to say about others and see less negative behaviour in them. We start seeing our kindness to ourself, reflected back by those around us. The kinder our inner voice is when we are thinking about ourself, the kinder the external environment becomes.

Chapter 26

# THE CIRCLE OF INFLUENCE AND THE CIRCLE OF CONCERN

Do you spend your day worrying about things, that on reflection, you can do nothing about but find it a challenge to stop thinking about them? Do you find it hard to let go of such thoughts? Here is a tool, via a visualisation, to assist with letting go of thoughts that we can do nothing about and give more productive thought to what we can do something about.

Let's imagine in front of us a circle and within that circle it is like a void, a hole that has no bottom and if we threw something into it, it would disappear completely. This is called the circle of concern. Now imagine a bigger circle out from the first circle and this circle, from the edge of the first circle, to this second circle is like a pin board that you can stick sticky notes on. This is the circle of influence.

Now that we have the image of the circle of concern, the inner circle and the circle of influence, the outer circle, the pin board, let's use them to assist us to reduce worrying about things we can't do anything about.

Our minds are very busy and we often have thoughts that are annoying, seem pointless or just won't go away. Each time we have a thought about something we are worrying about, we can ask ourself this question, 'Is this something I can influence, is there something I can do about it?' If the answer is no, then it is something we are concerned about but not something we can influence. To hold onto worrying thoughts, that we are unable to do anything about, is a waste of our thinking and our time. Using the visualisation of the circle of influence and the circle of concern, imagine seeing the thought we are concerned about as writing on a piece of paper in our head and visually pull the piece of paper out of our head, screw it up and throw it into the circle of concern and watch it disappear into infinity, never to return. There is no point giving excessive thought to something we can't do anything about, let it go and change the thoughts to something we can do something about.

If we ask ourself the same question, 'Is this something I can influence?' and the answer is yes, ask a second question, 'Is it something I can influence right now?' If the answer is 'yes', take the opportunity in that moment and do something about it, this stops the worry because action is being taken to do something about what we were worrying about. If the answer is 'no, I can't do anything about it right now', imagine writing the issue down on a sticky note, adding when it is able to be actioned and sticking the note on the circle of influence on the pinboard. (The action can also be put in our diary, once we have sorted the appropriate time it is going to be actioned, this cements the action.) What this does, is allows us to separate what we are concerned about and lighten up about what we can influence, by determining when we can action it. When the time is appropriate for us to take action on the sticky note that we stuck on the circle of influence, that we could not action immediately, we remove the sticky note and perform the action.

The circle of concern and the circle of influence can be visualised at any time they are needed and moved into the background when they are not needed. Just knowing they are there can quieten the mind and lessen the worry.

*Stephen Covey: 7 habits of Highly Effective People 1989*

## Chapter 27

# COMMUNICATION, THE WRITTEN AND SPOKEN WORD AND BODY LANGUAGE

In society today, the art of communication has been lost. The use of mobile phones, the internet and social media has changed the way people communicate.

Who texts all the time? Who has had an argument over a text communication (or an email), where it has been miss interpreted by the receiver? Have you miss interpreted a message sent to you? I have known of relationships to break up over poor communication via texting.

The written word is only approximately 7% of communication. We attach emotion to that text. If we are feeling the emotion of anger when reading the text, we can read the text through that emotion, changing the context of the message. If we are reading another's text with negative beliefs and emotional issues that we feel towards that person, we can interpret the message with those beliefs and emotions, creating a misinterpretation of the content of the message. Without the tonality of the verbal voice and body language to get a full picture of what is being communicated, the true meaning can be lost or distorted. We interpret through our own set of filters. Our filters are made up of our experiences and what we made them mean, our beliefs about ourself and others and the emotions attached. The beliefs and emotions can be positive or negative. If the beliefs and emotions are negative such as feelings like rejection, frustration, jealousy, anger, resentment and abandonment the outcome of the interpretation is usually distorted and biased against the sender.

There may be an error in the message due to a typing error or auto correct, the person sending the message has not picked up. This all leads to miss communication and often causes irreparable damage to relationships and friendships.

The spoken word is approximately 38% of communication. When we are talking to someone over the phone, we are picking up the tone they are using, as well as the words they are saying and this tells us more about what they are communicating and the emotions and feelings behind the words. There can be less chance of miss communication when we hear the tone they are using in their voice and the way they are speaking, plus the words they are using.

Body language is 55% of communication. How someone is standing, arms crossed, relaxed, pointing a finger, not looking us in the eye, open gesture or smiling, etc, is giving a more complete picture of the meaning and context of the communication, especially when it is combined with what they say and how they say it.

When we are hearing how the words are being communicated and seeing the body language, our interpretation of what is being said, is more likely to be what the person is trying to convey.

When we only have the written word, the interpretation is dependent on our emotional and mental state of being at the time, how we feel about the person sending the written message and what we want to make it mean, which can be very different from what the person is wanting to convey. Add in, the need to be right, driven by our beliefs, we will find evidence in the communication, to show us, we are right about the other person and it usually has negative connotations. This can happen even if we are using body language and verbal communication if we are not conscious and self-aware but at least we have the opportunity to interpret the incoming information using more of our senses (our reality) with discernment.

What would the best way to communicate with someone be? The best way is in person, face to face. When we communicate face to face, we get to use body language and verbal communication, along with tonality, hearing the way someone is delivering their words.

We get to look them in the eye and actually see them, feel them and create intimacy (IN TO ME SEE) with them, something that is missing in society today. We live in such a fast pace world, very few people take the time to just 'BE' with another person. I see the effect this has on intimate relationships between couples and within families. I sometimes ask my clients when was the last time you took the time to sit down with your partner and make continual eye contact with them, looking into each other's eyes and connecting (the right eye is the window to the soul)? They usually say never or a very long time. If we are not present, in the moment, conscious and self-aware a void grows and disconnection occurs. How can we expect to maintain intimacy (IN TO ME SEE) if we are not prepared to take the time to truly connect with those we love? Spending time with another, gives us the opportunity to fully connect and be present.

Connection via communication is so important because many people feel separated, lonely or alone, even when they are in an intimate relationship. One of the reasons we are here is to remove the separation that has occurred and create group consciousness, coming together as a family and community to create support and be of service to each other. It starts with good communication, being physically present and being conscious and self-aware.

# Chapter 28

# CREATING BETTER SLEEP

Who gets to the end of their day and gets into bed and then lays there thinking about all that happened or didn't happen during the day? Who beats themselves up with harsh judgements about what they did or didn't do throughout their day? Who has unkind thoughts and feelings about those they interacted with? Who has the same thoughts going around and around in their head, pushing sleep further and further away?

If we can deal with the thoughts, in a productive way, rather than trying to just not think about them, we can clear our mind faster and more powerfully.

We can ask ourselves three things.

What did I do well?

What didn't I do well?

How can I improve?

Having a journal or pad of paper and pen next to the bed to write out the answers, can be very productive to quieten the mind before bed. Getting the thoughts and the feelings out of our head and onto a piece of paper can be surprisingly effective to quieten the mind.

Asking the questions, in the order they are written, is like doing a review of our day. Asking ourself, what we did well, allows us to review the day and reward ourself with thoughts of positivity and gives ourself, a well-deserved, pat on the back. There is always something we can find in our day that has either gone well or taught us something, if we are open to learning and growing within ourself.

The second question, 'What didn't I do well?', is an opportunity to look at ourself inwardly and take notice of how we did not care for our mental, emotional and physical bodies within the experiences of the day. It is an opportunity to see where we were not being kind, mindful and harmless to others and to ourself. It is not a beat-up session to put ourself or others down. Be kind and come from an objective point of view, when consciously looking at where we didn't do well.

Now with the third question 'How can I improve?', we create the opportunity to look inward and see where we can shift what did not work for us and choose something positive and productive, so we don't repeat what we didn't do well again. Each time we repeat something that does not work for us, we will keep getting a result we do not want. It is only in our ability to change our inner environment, who we are being, letting go of what is not serving us, so we can experience a different external reflection. Energy follows our thoughts. In the changing of our thoughts, in the letting go, we get closer to finding our true self.

When we let go of the over thinking, at the end of the day, (well anytime really) we find more peace and calm, which in turn creates freedom in our life, giving us a more peaceful life and restful sleep.

## Chapter 29

# LIFE IS A GAME

Life is like a game of tennis.

Let's use our imagination, our visualising skills and imagine in front of us a tennis court and next to the court is a stand where people can watch the game. Where do you play life? Are you on the court with a racquet in your hand ready to play or are you in the stand watching life pass you by, not engaging opportunities or stretching out of your comfort zone? Often when we don't engage fully in our own life, we are inclined to engage in the lives of others and make negative judgements on how they are doing their life. We can become very critical of how other people choose to live their lives.

If the game of tennis represents your life, where do you want to be doing your life, in the stand or on the court? When I use this technique, near the end of the first session with my client's, they always say they want to play the game of their life on the court and not in the stand. We can't play our game of life if we are in the stand, we must be on the court to play the game of life. If you now realise you have been playing life in the stand, instead of on the court, using the ability of visualisation and imagination, let's visualise ourself, getting up, leaving the stand and walking onto the tennis court. Now we are all on the court let's look at how the Game of life works.

In the game of life who is our opponent? Remember external competition is very destructive. We can only really compete against ourself, so in the game of life our opponent, up the other end of the court is ourself, we play ourself in the game of life, looking to get to know ourself on a deeper level, to uncover who we really are and all our hidden talents and gifts.

In this game of tennis, representing the game of life, we have endless balls and endless games, till the moment we leave the human experience and if we get angry and throw our racquet, another racquet instantly appears in our hand.

Each time we serve a ball we are creating a new experience. If we hit a winning serve the experience may be over quickly. If we end up having a marathon, with lots of play back and forth over the tennis net, the experience lasts longer and can be tiring and a hard challenge. We may even lose the point and feel defeated. This is how life is. Our life is filled with experiences, experiences that test us, experiences that feel wonderful and experiences that are challenging and overwhelming. Some last a long time, others only a short time, just like the points in tennis.

Then we have the tennis games, each game is made up of points. This represents how our life experiences can come together and create a larger experience. We can lose some games and feel like life is playing hard ball. If we don't do something different and play a different way to win some points, we can lose a game. Maybe there is something we are not learning. We are being given opportunities to learn, to change what doesn't work, let go of old behaviours and habits and create what works, perhaps a new swing or change the way we hold the racquet or serve the ball. We win some points and games and we lose some points and games. But do we really lose if we are playing against ourself. Each time we engage in playing, we create the opportunity to learn our lessons, learn about ourself and who we are. Tennis pros study their opponents for hours so they know how to play against them. They also study themselves to see how they can improve their game. If we take the time to study ourself and go within, we can create an amazing game of life. The more we observe ourself and increase our perspective and self-awareness of how we are being in our life, we create opportunities to let go of what no longer serves us. If we hit a bad shot, we can take that experience and choose not to repeat it, we practice and perfect our game, learning as we go. When we hit a winning shot, we can repeat it and even improve on it.

Life is a game and we are here to play it. Sometimes we need to laugh at life when we are struggling, find an amusing way to look at it and be kind to ourself. There are more points and more games. Remember we are just practising being a human being trying to master it.

Tennis can be played socially at a picnic, just for fun, so lighten up and play to enjoy the game, see the lighter side of life, we are here to have some fun.

Who wants to play the game of life? Ok let's play.

Chapter 30

# THE BLOCK OF WOOD

Imagine when we come onto the planet, we are like a block of wood cut from the trunk of a very large tree. Inside the block of wood is the sculpture of our perfect self, yet there is all of this extra wood stopping us from seeing the sculpture of ourself within the block of wood. Our perfect self is already there with everything we need, yet to find ourself we need a hammer and a set of chisels to chip away at all that we are not, until we are left with our perfect self, the sculpture of ourself.

The process of letting go (chipping away) of all we are not, is the process of being a human being, growing, learning and evolving. To discover our true self is the goal of life. Each time we let go of a way of being, a behaviour or pattern of behaviour, that does not serve us in a positive way, we uncover more of our gifts and talents that we already have, that can now assist us to get in touch with our true self.

Sometimes the lesson is a big one and really obvious and we can chisel off a large piece of wood with a large chisel. Other times the lesson is trickier to see and we have to chip away gently, little bit by little bit, using a small chisel. Each time we chip away a little more of what we are not, we get to see a different world reflected back at us. The clearer we see ourself, the clearer is our reflection. The more we connect with the love that we are and the more love we have for others, seeing ourself as 'perfection in practice', as we try to master being a human being, the closer we are to freedom and peace.

When working with a client, I ask them to hand over the whip they whip themselves with and replace their whip with a hammer and set of chisels, using the block of wood analogy to show them that they have the tools and the free will to create themselves and their life. We have all we need within us and by letting go of the negative patterns and self-sabotaging behaviours, chipping them away, we uncover our true potential, our personal power, our strengths, gifts and talents.

My request is that we all break our self-flagellating whip in two and never use it on ourselves again and replace it with a hammer and set of chisels and we become the sculpturer of our own life, gently chipping away all we are not to find our magnificent self.

Chapter 31

# HOW TO MANIFEST AN AMAZING FUTURE

Our past has made us who we are **now**. Everything we have experienced in our past, including all our thoughts and be**lie**fs has sculpted and moulded us into the human being we are in this present moment. There is a big difference between be**lie**ving, our be**lie**fs and **know**ing. Be**lie**ving is still trying to convince ourselves about what ever it is we are thinking about and it is often distorted and/or made up from our perception and personal reality. **Know**ing comes from the depth of our being, is unshakable and is a **know**ing in every cell of our body. It is a trust we hold within ourself for ourself and our journey as a human **Be**ing. When we **know** it brings us into the **now,** this is where we manifest from.

What we think in the present moment (including our be**lie**fs about ourself or our **know**ing about ourself and others and our environment), gives us our future because 'energy follows thought'.

This means, we have the ability to create our future or at least a lot of what happens in it. Our future really doesn't exist because we can't live in it, it is only the thoughts and be**lie**fs about our possible future that exist. We have many possibilities in our future because we have a certain amount of free will. How do you want to use your free will to manifest an amazing future? We have this free will, yet very often we don't use it, or we use it in a negative way. Most be**lie**ve that what happens 'to' us creates our life, yet as the observer, we hold the key to the creation of our life. It's our thoughts and be**lie**fs or k**now**ing in the **now** moment, both conscious and unconscious, that draws our experiences towards us and this is how we create our future. We are the observer and creator of our life. I feel there is also universal timing, meaning 'our' timing and universal timing (associated with the 'PLAN') can be different. This can affect when something may happen. If there is a lesson we need to learn, this can also determine how the future shows up because we are learning via our experiences, especially through our relationships.

Remember we are the product in this moment of everything that has happened in our past and all we have learnt from our past experiences. This means, that what we think in this moment is going to have an effect on what we experience in our future. Each thought, be**lie**f or k**now**ing in each new moment, is how we create our future experiences. Our negative thoughts and be**lie**fs are created from the negative patterns we are here to let go of, related to our lessons and our evolution. If we spend our time in negative thoughts about our future, (which usually manifest as anxiety) we will create negative experiences in that future, that we live in to. The faster we shift to a positive state of **know**ing, the easier it is to manifest an amazing life. So many times, when working with clients, they shift their thoughts and be**lie**fs about themselves and others, to a positive state of **know**ing in the session, which is in the present moment, in the **now**. They do this, by becoming more conscious and aware of themselves and taking responsibility for how they created their life. When they come to their next session, they tell me that their experiences with others, particularly family members and partners, has shifted to a much more positive experience, yet the other person has not had a therapy session. By shifting to a positive **know**ing about themselves and letting go of old thinking and be**lie**fs, they no longer get the negative reflection from those they are in relationships with. In the moment, by seeing themselves and the world they live in, in a positive light, they manifest a more positive future. We can manifest in every moment of our life.

To manifest what we want, we need to **know** in every cell of our body, that we already have what it is we want in our life. I am not only talking about material things, I am also talking about what most people want in their life, which I feel is to love and to be loved, to be free and at peace, to have their life filled with kindness, laughter, joy, harmony and connection and to feel included and be a part of something bigger than themselves? When we **know** our life is already filled with love (and self love) and connection, peace, freedom and harmony the details of how that shows up, we can let go of because when we **know** it is already in existence, the details take care of themselves, that is how manifesting works because of our connection to source. Many people don't know what they want and have no idea of what would make them happy. One of the ways to discover what makes us happy is to shift our thoughts and emotions to a positive state and trust, by doing this, we are led in the perfect direction to a positive outcome.

Our positive thoughts and k**now**ing, plus our emotional state and visions of what we want need to all be aligned to manifest. We need to k**now** we deserve it by having loving, positive and kind thoughts about ourself. If our inner critic is active in our mental body, which in turn effects our emotional body negatively, then the ability to manifest a positive future is unlikely to happen. Everything needs to be aligned towards positivity. We need to k**now** that what we want is already manifested, already in existence, we have it in our life **now**. This is the key to manifesting, seeing it already in action in our life. It is like we can use our five senses to see it, hear it, touch it, taste it and smell it, whichever are appropriate towards what we are manifesting. We can write about, (it must be in the present tense) draw it, see it in our dreams and visualise it. The more we can sense and feel that it is already happened in the present moment, the stronger our ability to manifest it. We can create our future by what we think in the present moment. Remember we are the observer of our life and the creator.

People often view what is happening in their external world and don't like it, holding onto the negative they see and hear and continually talk about it, reliving it and tell others about it. If we keep thinking and talking about something in the present moment, whether it be positive or negative, we can attract more of it just by holding on to thoughts and putting it out into the world with our words. What would a better way be to contribute to manifesting an amazing world? Think and visualise the world as we want to see it, already filled with kindness, love, peace and freedom.

Choose wisely what we take in through social media, television, newspapers and movies, gossip etc. If it is mainly negative, overly dramatic, violent and not want we want in our life, (and not the real truth) then that is what holds us in a state of negativity and fear. When we drop into our heart space and think from our heart, we will find our truth and what is right for ourselves and our highest good. There is so much to be positive about, the more we think in a positive way and **know** we have peace, kindness, love, self love and freedom in our life already, the more of it we manifest.

Chapter 32

# HOW TO LOVE OURSELF

Many a client has said to me, 'How do I love myself, I don't know how'? The one lesson we all pick when we come into a human body is to learn to love ourself. When I ask, what is the hardest thing to learn, most say it is to love themselves.

Let's recap on how we sabotage ourself, preventing us from loving ourself. We criticise and judge ourself, destroying our self-worth, and often our life, because it destroys the relationship we have with ourself, which in turn destroys the relationships we have with others. If we are someone who criticises others, remember, what we think of someone else is our own reflection of how we feel and think about ourself, that we are not yet conscious of.

We compete outside of ourself, by comparing ourself with others. As soon as we compare ourself with something or someone else we set up an inner conflict, a war that rages, often out of control, effecting our mental and emotional wellbeing.

We give ourself bad advice, advice that usually is detrimental to our inner being because the advice is related to what we think we need to do or be in our external world for others approval or recognition and to have others love us.

What is love? Esoterically, as to the part love plays in our healing process: Love is the life expression of God Himself; love is the coherent force which makes all things whole, and love is all that *is*. In our ability to heal ourself we are making ourself whole. We are working towards actualising our human potential by balancing our personality, our mental, emotional and physical bodies so our soul can control our outer form, life and all events. When we have a balanced personality, love is more able to be given and received. All there is, is love. Self love is our greatest lesson to learn.

The first relationship we have is the one we have with ourself. It is the longest relationship we have. It starts the moment we are born and ends the moment we leave our body on our death bed. It is the relationship that needs to be worked on first, before any others, as the impact it has on our external relationships is profound. We are here to create right human relationships with ourself and then with others.

Establishing a loving relationship with ourself, means we need to act for our own highest good and find our truth, by putting ourself first. This allows us to make healthy choices from within, rather than from what is happening in our external world. Some may see this as selfish but it is the opposite because if we are acting for our highest good, what we give out is of the highest calibre to others. As within as without.

Esoteric Healing: Alice Bailey, Page 356

We need to think with our heart and feel with our head, instead of thinking with our head and feeling with our heart. When we think from our heart, our emotional brain, we make better choices. The monkey mind can lead us astray, whereas heart centred thinking allows us to create heartfelt thoughts, which are generally kinder and more mindful. When we feel with our mind, it allows us to feel what the thoughts are and how they affect us emotionally. It opens up our emotional body and our self-awareness to be gentle with our thoughts towards ourself and others. It is a much more loving way to listen to ourself. Ponder and reflect, for as a "man thinketh *in his heart,* so is he".

Loving ourself, is setting boundaries that are for our highest good. Learning to say 'no' and not having to defend our 'no', freely being able to choose what serves our life in a positive way. Good boundaries come from setting appropriate limits for ourself, which enhances our ability to make good and fair judgement for ourself and others, while being grounded and centred. Knowing ourself and our patterns, gives us the strength to push against the boundaries that limit us and the boundaries that cause us to be taken advantage of. Loving ourself enough to put healthy boundaries in place, creates balance in our life. It is the action of creating the boundaries that shows up as loving one's self.

Esoteric Psychology Volume 1:<br>Alice Baily A Treatise on The Seven Rays page 430

# The Gold Mine To Consciousness

Loving ourself is listening to our thoughts and letting go of the negative ones, knowing that we are much more than our thoughts. It is finding the thoughts that praise us and build us up, creating loyalty and respect to our humanness and the journey we are undertaking. We choose our thoughts. Making the commitment to choose positive, loving, kind and mindful thoughts about ourself, is incredibly empowering. It assists us to align our life, so we draw in those that are of the same positive, loving frequency. What we are and who we are being, goes out into the world and is reflected back to us in our relationships.

Trust ourself and our own intuition, that we know deep down, what is best for ourselves, our deep knowing. Learning to use our intuition, creates trust in our own process of life, which only we can live. The more we use our intuition, the stronger it becomes and the more we trust it. Our intuitive brain is our third brain, which is our whole digestive system from our mouth to our anus. When people say 'I had a gut feeling about that', they are talking about their intuitive brain their digestive system. The stomach is where we digest and assimilate a lot of our life experiences, it is associated with our conscious mind. People who have gut problems are usually living an unconscious life. Being self-aware and conscious assists to heal the digestive system. Loving ourself, is knowing and trusting that we are exactly where we need to be for our growth and development. Life unfolds perfectly, trusting the process assists us to be light and kind, as we move along on our life journey.

BodyTalk Fundamentals: by Dr. John Veltheim & Sylvia Muiznieks

Acceptance of ourself just as we are, remembering we are here 'practising trying to master being a human being' and the journey is not always smooth. It is the catalysts and difficulties in our life, that are giving us the best opportunities to learn our life lessons. As we learn and let go of old limiting beliefs and ways of being with self-acceptance, it allows us to find new ways of being, our hidden gifts and talents to make life easier. As we accept ourself just as we are, in each moment, we are loving ourself a little more.

When we show up in our own life with courage and integrity, we are loving ourself enough to be present. When we are taking responsibility and embracing our strengths and weaknesses, we are loving ourself. Love is being there for ourselves, showing that we support ourself and have faith in who we are, with our individuality, that is our divine right. Respect and compassion for ourself is loving one's self. Each time we value ourself and trust that all our experiences are moving us to unlock our fullest potential, (that is always within us) we are loving ourself a little more.

Gaining a bigger perspective of ourself, in our life, allows us to be more objective as we move through experiences and situations. Seeing a bigger picture gives us a more balanced view and we are usually gentler with ourselves. I find when we view life from a bigger perspective, we are more detached (detachment = caring deeply from an objective place) and kinder to ourself, less judgemental and this reflects more love of self.

Love is the kindness and compassion we show ourself. Love is acceptance of who we are, our life and all the experiences we draw to ourself, that give us the opportunity to learn more about who we are. Love is acknowledging the negatives our mental body chooses to think and overriding them, instead choosing positive, reinforcing thoughts with our sense of deep knowing who and what we are. Love is knowing that all the good behaviours and qualities we see in others, are able to be seen because we too have the same good qualities.

Love is being able to give and receive equally. If we are only able to give, we are being a martyr. If we love ourself, we are able to receive from others because we give to ourself. This is the reflection at work. People often ask or wish for something but it won't manifest if we don't think we are worthy of receiving it.

Love is taking care of the physical body, what we eat and drink, keeping it clean and healthy, dressing it well, nurturing it every day and treating the vehicle, we do our life in, our body, with the respect that it deserves, it has to last us for as long as we are on the planet, we don't have a spare body to replace it with when it malfunctions from our lack of love for it, so love every part of it.

Love is looking after our emotional body, allowing ourself to feel. We have an emotional body for a reason. We usually don't want to feel the negative emotions so we shut our emotional body down with drugs, food and any number of other ways. Yet in shutting the emotional body down it means we usually don't get to feel the positive emotions either, we are too drugged causing us to be out of our body. Balance is the key. Loving all the emotions and feelings, means we get the opportunity to feel all the wonderful feelings of joy, bliss, contentment, peace, freedom, compassion, harmony, fulfillment and of course self love and love. We can only feel these emotions in the now, in the moment we are in, so being present, conscious and self-aware gives us the great privilege of living a life filled with our own divinity and beauty.

Love ourself by being patient, as we travel our human journey, become our own biggest supporter by praising ourself as often as possible. We have no idea how powerful we truly are.

Know what we want and spend time doing the things that we love to do. Use our natural creative talents in any area of our life, we all have them, it is up to us to explore what they are. Make what we love a business then it comes to us naturally. Fall in love with the feeling, that is created when we are doing what we love, our body will love us for it and stay healthier and even heal.

Laughter is the best medicine, whether it be at a movie, at ourself (only in a positive way) or at what life presents us. Find the funny and light side of situations. The cells, that make up our physical body, respond to the lightness of laughter in a positive way.

If we pressurise ourself and leave no time to recharge, meditate and relax, especially in nature, we lose our spark and life force. Love is taking time out to recharge and refocus on ourself to keep our cup full. Our ability to balance our physical, emotional and mental bodies so we can connect with our soul and our higher mind is extremely important for our evolution.

I have only touched the surface of ways to love ourself. It is a choice. We only have to choose self-love, put it into practice, and practice some more and possibly even more, till we build a big muscle of self love. Be self-loving by taking action. Start with something small and action it. Action something each day. Keep building more and more self love by actioning loving thoughts and emotions. Do something different that feels loving, kind and generous. It is after all called SELF love, no one can give us self love, no matter how much they profess their love for us or to us, it is an inner experience. Self love is the most empowering quality we can develop as a human being because in loving ourself we can only give and receive what we are, love!

Never underestimate the effect our self love has on others, it is contagious, like the pebble thrown in the pond that creates ripples that go out, our effect reaches far and wide, much farther than we could ever imagine.

Imagine a world where every single person loved themselves. All the reflections would be love, we would have no need for duality and we would have heaven on earth.

Chapter 33

# TRUE SERVICE

What is true service? For what reasons would we want to be of service to another? When we are of service to others, do we expect something for our service?

I believe we are able to be of true service when we are heart centred, have love for ourself and others and have developed love-wisdom. It is through our contact with each other, our relationships and experiences that we create the opportunity to love. Once we develop love through understanding, inclusiveness and identification of ourself in the relationships we have, we develop wisdom through self-awareness of what is required within each relationship and use our ability to know what is needed and how to meet that need. Service is the expression of love-wisdom.

Esoteric Astrology: Alice Bailey, Page 494.

The Esoteric definition of service is, The utilisation of soul force for the good of the group. To me, this means as we balance our physical, emotional and mental bodies and have more control over our personality, we align with our soul and our personal desires become less important as we see a greater cause, that of the betterment of humanity. Our true individual purpose gets activated. I see service as the ultimate expression of the love we have found for ourself and others playing out in the mundane world. It can show up from the smallest act of service to the greatest of humanitarian endeavours.

Service can be expressed in many ways. Most people have no realisation they are being of service. Serving our family can be as simple as showing up when a family member is struggling. Just our presence can be supportive and an act of service, remembering they are not broken and don't need fixing, they are having an experience giving them the opportunity to go within and let go and learn about themselves. Allowing them to lead the situation and letting them know we are present and available if they need us, is being of service. Service to our family, is usually how we first action being of service. For children the family pet can teach them how to be of service, feeding, walking, brushing, giving loving cuddles all are being of service to the wellbeing of the family pet.

Our relationship with a partner gives us the opportunity to be of service. A simple way is asking if there is anything we can do for them or do they need anything from us. Many people do not realise they are usurping another's opportunity to learn by trying to fix the situation or taking over or tell them what to do, rather than be detached, (caring deeply from an objective point of view) allowing the person to move through their experience, learning as they go. No one likes to be told what to do, so asking open questions (questions that allow the person to find their own answer, not being told what to do within the question) to gain a better perspective of the situation, for all involved, is a way of being of service. Using gentleness and kindness, allowing room for the person struggling, to find their answers within the questions asked. Being of service is allowing someone the room to see themselves in their life, seeing what works and what doesn't, holding space for them and showing up supportive and loving.

Being of service in our community can be as simple as picking up litter as we go for a walk or asking someone who may be struggling with their shopping trolly if they need some help. The opportunities are endless to be of service by asking if another would like some assistance. Asking is the key! On a larger scale there are many individuals and companies that work tirelessly with in their community to be of service. Volunteers are the backbone of a community, by providing service in many sectors. My father volunteered at Meals on Wheels in his local community, until he needed the service himself. Many retirees give continued service in their communities, without them many would suffer. I see this in those that serve the animal kingdom, saving, protecting, caring and rehabilitating those that have been abused, mis-placed and injured.

There are others that serve by assisting mother earth, protecting her resources and the environment, water, air, soil, minerals and plant life. Here there is an endless supply of ways of being of service.

# The Gold Mine To Consciousness

Group consciousness is something that was introduced to humanity after World War II as an experiment, by those who know the PLAN to see how humanity would respond. Many people are drawn to groups to be of service. A group is three or more people and they do not have to be in the same place. Due to technology, many groups who are of service, are scattered all over the world, connected by their common desire to be of service in a particular area. This is group consciousness at work.

As group consciousness is an experiment there are groups who are not aligned with heart centred service. We see this playout as self-serving or sheep mentality, those following someone who does not have love for humanity and the planet as their focus, instead it is usually driven by greed and control. The dark side can be very deceiving, playing both sides to create a win for them. Always use discrimination and look deeply, what and who are behind what is being presented.

As we evolve and become more conscious and self-aware, both individually and as a race, we create the opportunity to activate our heart centre. The heart energy when activated brings about inclusivity. Remember as a "man thinketh *in his heart,* so is he". The more our heart centre is activated the more we are able to serve from a place of good will and the will-to-good takes over, which is the first steps towards love, right human relations and peace. Service saves, liberates and releases the imprisoned consciousness. Service is to be applied in the spirit of love.

Esoteric Healing: Alice Bailey, page 441, Page 160

# CONCLUSION

I have experienced so much joy in writing this book. I see this book as one of my contributions to assist others to actualise their human potential by finding the love that they are innately and see that love expressed out into the world. The strength of a person is defined by how much they love themselves, the tougher the life, the more strength of mind it takes to love one's self.

If we are made in the image of God and God is the creator, then we too are creators of our own life. My desire is that this book has given each person that reads it, the will to look within, let go of anything that is not loving towards themselves and others and create a life deserving of the magnificence that we all are.

Shine the light that is within, out into the world, so it brightens all of humanity. Love and kindness are contagious, let's pay it forward and infect as many people as possible with divine love and love wisdom.

I would like to conclude with a Myth I wrote, showing that each one of us, together, make up humanity and we have the opportunity to save humanity and the earth when we serve together as one.

## The Window of Humanity

Once upon a time there was a beautiful window in an old castle. It faced towards the afternoon sun and the sun's rays streamed in, lighting and warming the room where books of great wisdom and knowledge were read by those wanting to learn. This room was a very important room and many great scholars came to the room to write, adding new knowledge and profound wisdom to this wonderful room. The window had a beautiful leadlight pane at the top and when the sunlight streamed in it would cast glorious colours into the room. Those that came into the room, would place their chair, so the sun's rays that entered through the window would warm them as they read. The window gleamed, knowing it was the source of light making the reading of wisdom and knowledge a joy for those that entered the room. As the books were opened and read the window could absorb all the knowledge and store it within its beautiful coloured glass pane.

Over time, the window found it was less interested by what was happening inside the room and more intrigued by what was happening outside. It could see people playing games, children laughing and families picnicking under beautiful big trees. It looked like everyone was having fun. The window was enjoying absorbing all the fun and laughter that was happening outside and storing it in its lead light pane.

One day, the window noticed a couple, who seemed to be enjoying their picnic, until suddenly voices started to be raised and they were yelling at each other. Fingers were being pointed and accusations were being made, tears were being shed. The couple were pushing each other and becoming violent and others joined in and started fighting. Now the window is not only seeing what is happening but is also feeling it, as it absorbs all that surrounds it and stores it in its lead light pane. The scene out of the window was becoming more and more stressful, the black anger was too much for the window to cope with, so it started to darken to block it out. Slowly, the beautiful window turned black and no sunlight entered the reading room. Scholars no longer came to write their words of wisdom and knowledge and the books were left to collect dust on the shelf. The beautiful lead light pane at the top of the window could no longer absorb knowledge and wisdom.

The window started to realise, that by wanting to spend too much time in the mundane world outside, it had cut off its source of growth and learning. It had stopped being of service to those that it could help, the scholars and the readers of knowledge and wisdom that came into the reading room. It had veered from its path and now its world was cold, dark and painful.

What had it learnt from those books of wisdom and knowledge? What did it now need to draw from to get its gleam back? It had wisdom and knowledge stored in its lead light pane, now it needed to use this wisdom and knowledge for itself. As the window started to pull from its stored knowledge it gained strength. It knew it needed to change, so it gathered all its power and strength and imploded, shattering the central clear glass pane into many pieces, while keeping the lead light pane in place, so as not to lose all the wisdom and knowledge others had so kindly given it.

The window was replaced with new glass that again gleamed. The lead light pane was buffed and cleaned, sending rays of colour into the room, once again letting in the warm golden sunlight into the reading room to allow all those that entered to sit in its warmth to write and study. Down each side of the window, a new leadlight pane was added, so the window could absorb more knowledge and wisdom and forever keep a more balanced view of the two worlds it had the privilege to witness, the world of the mundane, outside and the world of wisdom, knowledge and growth from inside so it could continue its inner journey.

# APPENDIX

Astrology for the Soul: Jan Spiller, published 1997 by Bantam Dell a division of Random House, Inc New York Jan Spiller's website: www.janspiller.com

Your Drug or Your Life, Prescriptions for getting clear: Ruby Johnson, published 2002 by Transformational Enterprises. Ruby Johnson's website: www.wholisticpsychonomy.com

Being Born, How your birth affects your learning performance, lifestyle and relationships: Robyn Fernance, published 2003 by Inner Connections Australia. Robyn Fernance's website: www.breathandinspiration.com/robyn-fernance-being-born.html (book available in digital format from the website)

The Secret Language of your Body, the essential guide to health and wellness: Inna Segal, published 2007 by Blue Angel Publishing Australia. Inna Segal's website: www.innasegal.com

The Body is the Barometer of the Soul II, so be your own doctor: Annette Noontil, published 1994 by Gemcraft P/L Australia

Permanent Healing, includes quantum mechanics of healing: Daniel R. Condron, published 1992 by The school of Metaphysics USA

www.ingramcontent.com/pod-product-compliance
Lightning Source LLC
Chambersburg PA
CBHW050310010526
44107CB00055B/2178